From the
Darkest Places
Come the
Brightest Lights

*Reflections on Service, Faith, and Life
from the Co-Founder of Open Arms Home
for Children, South Africa*

Bob Solis

BALBOA.
PRESS
A DIVISION OF HAY HOUSE

Balboa Press books may be ordered through booksellers or by contacting:

Balboa Press
A Division of Hay House
1663 Liberty Drive
Bloomington, IN 47403
www.balboapress.com
1 (877) 407-4847

Print information available on the last page.

ISBN: 978-1-5043-4565-1 (sc)
ISBN: 978-1-5043-4567-5 (hc)
ISBN: 978-1-5043-4566-8 (e)

Library of Congress Control Number: 2015919803

Balboa Press rev. date: 1/19/2016

Dedication

This book is dedicated to my family. My wife, Sallie, is the bedrock of our family, and she made this story possible. Our five children, Alicia, Jaala, Lou Ann, Sammy, and Jonsy, have taught us how precious family can be and have inspired us to share that gift with others.

Contents

Foreword xi

Preface xiii

1. Can You Take Him? 1

2. My Favorite Thing 3

3. Words I'll Never Forget 5

4. Faith to Move Mountains 8

5. God in Khayelitsha 11

6. Motivation 13

7. The Rocking Chair 16

8. The Song 19

9. Do It Now 21

10. Thanks, Dad 23

11. A Letter from Bobo, Spring 2013 25

12. Hope 27

13. The Only Bible Some People Will Ever Read 28

14. Perspective 30

15. A Death in the Family 31

16. A Meaningful Prayer 33

17. A Great Truth 35

18. Long International Flights 37

19. Shoes 42

20. Under Starry Skies 44
21. Six Powerful Words 46
22. The End of the Road...49
23. An Eye-Opener 53
24. Life on the Edge...55
25. What You Do 58
26. Letta 60
27. Spiritual Poverty...62
28. Yin and Yang..65
29. Playing It Safe 69
30. A Letter from Bobo, Spring 2011 72
31. I Promise to Sing to You 74
32. Flour and Water 76
33. Father 78
34. Generosity..80
35. An Awesome Responsibility.......................................82
36. Loaves and Mattresses 85
37. Never...87
38. Callings..89
39. A Lot to Live Up To 91
40. Faith in Action 93
41. Winning the Lottery 96
42. A Letter from Bobo, Fall 2010 98
43. Bobby..100
44. Imagine..102
45. The Universal Language...104
46. The Start..106
47. The Tension..108
48. Woe Is Me—Not! 110
49. Lessons Learned on the Road 112
50. Luck? 116
51. A Day at a Time 119
52. The Start of the Day 122
53. The Children of God 124

54. Religion 127

55. In Our Darkness 129

56. Too Much 131

57. Good Tired.. 134

58. The Hospice.. 137

59. Heart.. 140

60. Bert's Buses 142

61. A Child Is Born 146

62. Faith to Move Anthills 148

63. The River 150

64. If You Want to Walk on Water.................... 154

65. Service Above Self 157

66. A Letter from Bobo, Spring 2012 161

67. Uncle John... 163

68. Travel 167

69. Time Is Not on Our Side, Ever.................... 169

70. A Letter from Bobo, Fall 2012.................... 171

71. You Never Know 173

72. American Eyes... 175

73. God Is With Us.. 177

74. The Why... 179

75. A Letter from Bobo, Spring 2010 183

76. South Bend 185

77. Lasting Joy 188

78. A Chance Occurrence?.............................. 190

79. The Spinner in the Sky.............................. 192

80. Full Surrender 194

81. Two Words 196

82. Challenges.. 199

83. The Rainbow Connection 200

84. One More Day...203

85. A Letter from Bobo, Fall 2013....................206

86. He's Gone 208

87. The Rock? 210

88. Our True Essence...212
89. At the Dump...215
90. Fear and Love...217
91. A Letter from Bobo, Spring 2014...............................218
92. The Gift of the Present.......................................220
93. The Main Thing...225
94. Like Riding a Bike...227
95. Getting Paid...229
96. Reflections..231
97. Connected..233
98. Who Was He?..236
99. The Last Chapter...238
Afterword..241
Sources..243

Foreword

I'm often asked about my life's journey from humble beginnings in the small town of Avondale, Arizona, to the bright lights of the National Football League and ultimately to the rarified air of the Pro Football Hall of Fame. My answer always leads me back to the difference makers in my life—the people who invested their time and energy in me as a young person—the people who believed in me before I believed in myself. Without them, my journey would not have happened. Because of those people and my personal experience, I'm a firm believer that it takes a village to raise a child.

When it comes to difference makers, I can think of no better examples than my high school friend Sallie Solis, her husband, Bob, and their five children. Fueled by strong Christian values and armed with the belief they could make a difference, this regular working family set out to change the lives of some of the smallest and most vulnerable souls affected by the realities of poverty and AIDS in South Africa.

The Solis family has quite literally created a village to raise children who have been orphaned, abandoned, or abused. The result of this remarkable journey is a magical place of hope and opportunity called the Open Arms Home for Children.

Thanks to a leap of faith from a family halfway around the world, the lives of fifty-seven children (and counting) have been filled with promise—their dreams rekindled, their destinies rewritten, their journeys made possible.

This story is as inspirational and miraculous as it is unlikely. It is truly a shining example of the power of one—that is, one family—to turn darkness into light.

However, the true stars of this story are the children themselves. Their strength, spirit, smiles, and resiliency provide life lessons for all of us. They are proof positive that *From the Darkest Places Come the Brightest Lights.*

The story of Open Arms Home for Children is a gift to all who read this book. You will be inspired, motivated, and empowered to find ways large and small to make an impact in your corner of the world.

It will leave you changed forever.

Randall McDaniel
Member, Pro Football Hall of Fame (2009)

Preface

Nearly ten years ago, my family embarked on a dream to start a home for orphaned children in South Africa. On the surface, it was a farfetched, crazy idea. How does a U.S. stockbroker and his family start a home for children orphaned by AIDS on the other side of the world? We had not run a home for children before. We were not wealthy by U.S. standards, and we had five children coming up on college at the time. To be honest, we needed every dollar we had saved. In so many ways, it was a ridiculous idea to start a project 11,000 miles away from our home in suburban Phoenix. But we believed then, and still do now, that God qualifies the called rather than calls the qualified. We weren't qualified for the job, but that didn't mean we couldn't do it.

The genesis of this project came on a family mission trip to South Africa in 2004. My wife, Sallie, and I had always wanted to show our children how the other half of the world lived, and so we went to work in an orphanage for a week in Johannesburg. After seeing so much need on that trip, we simply felt we could not turn away when we returned home. We asked ourselves: How can we sit and do nothing after seeing how many children had lost their parents to AIDS and had nowhere to live? In fact, on our family's trip, we saw so many children in need that we didn't think God was whispering to us to do something but rather hitting us with a two-by-four right on the forehead. St. Paul once wrote that we are to be "fools for Christ," and after our shared experience on vacation, we were convinced that the only foolish thing we could do was to do nothing at all.

Now ten years later, Open Arms Home for Children has more than fifty children who call us home. Witnessing the birth, growth, and maturation of this project has been a joy and a privilege. So many things have happened—too much to fill a short book. But the one constant has been the joy of serving Christ, as Mother Teresa once put it, "in all his distressing disguises." Children come to us from the direst circumstances and then invariably inspire us with their lives. It is a privilege to witness this.

If there is one reality that I have discovered in this wonderful journey, it is that from the darkest places come the brightest lights. Time and again, we have witnessed how people—and little ones at that—can soar to new heights after starting their lives in a very dark place. It is humbling to witness how sorrow can turn to joy and tragedy can transform into triumph. The resiliency of the human spirit is truly one of the most powerful forces in the world, and we have had front-row seats to see it.

This book is a compilation of thoughts, experiences, and reflections on one family's journey of faith, hope, and service. I have written it so I don't forget the lessons I have learned and to highlight some moments of this journey in which we have consistently found God where he is always present: in the service of others.

I hope that this book will provide three things to readers. First, I hope it helps those who read it learn of the power they have to make a difference. I firmly believe that God has given each of us a mission that is uniquely suited to our talents and abilities. It doesn't mean we have to go to a faraway land to fulfill it but merely to listen to that strong and silent voice within that says "go," whether "go" means down the street or across the world.

Second, I hope this book may help readers develop a sense of gratitude for the blessings that abound in our lives. The main characters of this book, orphaned children, lack much of what we take for granted. And yet they are thankful, spirited, and filled with joy. I hope that their collective humility and deep sense of gratitude will help inspire us all to count blessings that we often fail to notice.

And third, and perhaps most importantly, I hope this book will make evident that obstacles for others are only opportunities for us to serve. Our family's experience serving the least of our brothers and sisters has taught us, beyond a shadow of a doubt, that the brightest lights do indeed come from the darkest places.

May the peace and joy that comes from serving God and others be yours every single day of your life.

All the names of children in this book have been intentionally changed in order to protect the identities of individual children.

I slept and dreamt that life was joy.
I awoke and saw that life was service.
I acted and behold, service was joy.

Rabindranath Tagore

Grown men can learn from very little children for the hearts of the little children are pure. Therefore, the Great Spirit may show to them many things which older people miss.

Black Elk, Sioux Medicine Man

We can have a personal relationship with the Lord, but never an individual one. We go to God with our brothers and sisters or we don't go at all. He planned it this way, and we can't go with them unless we know and care for them, until there is no more strength or life in us.

Monsignor Jack Egan

If you want to go fast, go alone.
If you want to go far, go together.

African Proverb

1. Can You Take Him?

Shortly after our family's mission trip to South Africa in 2004, I made plans to return to South Africa to more fully investigate the HIV/AIDS problem and to visit several children's homes to see the various approaches to orphan care. On that visit, I was traveling across the Western Cape Province when I stopped at a roadside stand to get a soda. While purchasing a Coke, I started up a conversation with a local couple who had a twelve-year-old boy with them.

They asked, "What are you doing here in South Africa?"

I told them my family was thinking of opening a home for orphaned children, and I was in the country to investigate the possibilities.

Without skipping a beat, they pointed at the twelve-year-old boy and said, "Can you take him?"

To say that I was absolutely dumbfounded is an understatement. "Take him?" I asked.

"Yes, take him," they said.

They'd apparently found the boy somewhere, and he had no one to take care of him. They were feeding and caring for him until they could figure something out. When I came along, they thought they had a possible solution to their problem.

For his part, the boy spoke Xhosa and only knew a few words of English. But he certainly understood the words "Can you take him," for the moment he heard them, his eyes welled up with tears.

I simply could not believe what I was hearing or feeling—but even more importantly, I couldn't imagine what the boy was going through. It was too much for all of us.

Seeing that boy's eyes well up with tears and feeling so badly for that couple trying to do the right thing made me absolutely certain that Open Arms would one day exist. It was only a matter of time. How else could I live with the question "Can you take him"?

I don't think I will ever comprehend the reality of children who have absolutely no one to care for them. Since that day, I have met many children without parents who have no place to go. They are on their own at age three or five or ten. I struggle to run a household in my 50s. How can someone do it as a child?

You stop on the side of the road for two minutes to buy a Coke, and someone offers you a young boy because they don't know what to do with him. "Can you take him?" The words still echo in my ears and stir me in ways I can't fully explain.

2. My Favorite Thing

....

I go to Open Arms about three times a year to check in on things. I meet the new children, hug the ones who've been with us for years, visit with the staff and community leaders, and meet with our executive director. The visits are important to me for a lot of reasons, but mostly because it's critical that I know the children and their stories. Knowing their stories helps me to be their voice on this side of the Atlantic. I also think the visits are important for the kids, because I've been a constant presence in most of their lives for an extended period of time. We are family.

Because I have a full-time job here in the States, I usually leave Phoenix on a Saturday and get back home the following Sunday. The trips require a lot of sitting on my fanny in a coach seat on Delta Airlines for more than twenty-four hours each way. Even though I feel like a pretzel in those seats, the trips are worth it—especially once I get there.

In many ways, I am like a big kid. I thoroughly enjoy playing sports and games, climbing trees, and goofing around with kids. I especially love to do that at Open Arms, and the kids enjoy it too. I often say Open Arms is the happiest place on earth, because there's a lot of joy every day (my apologies to Disneyland, which probably has a copyright on the phrase). Soccer games, tag, arts and crafts, and bike riding are common activities that bring joy to our campus. But as much as I enjoy interacting with the children, there is one activity I like doing better. My favorite thing to do at Open Arms is to sit in a building or behind a tree and watch the children having fun. They are carefree, and they have just as much fun as I did as a child.

For kids who have had to deal with adult problems at young ages, I think the greatest gift Open Arms gives is the restoration of their childhoods. Many of our children have had to beg for food, care for dying adults, deal with abuse, move from place to place, and worry about surviving all of that—and more. Because of that, it is not unusual for children who first come to us to take some food at mealtime and put it in their pockets. They are not used to having regular meals, and they want to make sure they have food for later. It is both understandable and heartbreaking to see this.

Childhood only comes once for every human being. For most of us, it is a magical time, and we look back on it fondly. For children who have been orphaned, it is often a time of great pain and trauma. It is for this reason that the thing I like to do most at Open Arms is sit inside and watch the children play in the yard. Nothing gives me greater satisfaction or motivates me more to keep going.

What is Open Arms all about? You could say it's about hope or love or opportunity or any number of similar things. However, at its core, it's about children playing in the yard—children who aren't worried about a darned thing. For the kids—and for me too—nothing can beat that.

3. Words I'll Never Forget

On my first trip to South Africa by myself, I spent a week in the Cape Town area going to orphanages and townships to see how we might address the orphan problem in an effective way. For most of the week, I went to children's homes and talked with community leaders in order to get their opinions on the best way to serve children who'd lost their parents.

On the second-to-last night I was there, I decided to play tourist for a night, and I went to the V&A Waterfront, a large mall and restaurant area on Cape Town's harbor. After parking my car, I headed to the stairs to exit the parking garage. There, at the top of the stairs, I ran into two girls begging for money. I gave them some cash, but then, over the next two hours, I learned their stories.

Their names were Sumayah, age eighteen, and Adly, age sixteen. They were sisters who'd grown up in a township (we would call it a slum) on the outskirts of Cape Town. One night, a propane heater in their shack exploded, killing their mother and disabling their father. Sumayah was badly burned on the arm and chest. After this tragic event, the siblings' father was no longer able to work, and they lost their home. With no place to go, Sumayah and Adly suddenly found themselves living on the streets of Cape Town.

When I met them, they were living behind the parking structure where I'd just parked. It was the coldest month of the year, with very rainy conditions and temperatures often in the forties at night. To stay alive, Sumayah and Adly begged during the day and fended off men at night. It was a very difficult existence in every way. Sumayah had lost her front four teeth in a struggle with a man who wanted more than she was willing to give.

Sumayah and Adly were exactly the same ages as two of my three daughters back home. Their obvious love and concern for each other reminded me of my own wonderful daughters. After our conversation, I told the girls that the next night would be my last in Cape Town, and I would take them shopping at five p.m. We decided to meet at the top of the stairs in the parking garage.

Going shopping with Sumayah and Adly was great fun. I bought them what they needed: shoes, socks, undies, jeans, sweaters, jackets, and hats. They had a great time, but I enjoyed it even more than they did (and as my family knows, I hate shopping).

After we finished buying everything, I asked them if they wanted to go get something to eat. Adly, the younger sister, said she wanted to go show off her new wardrobe to her friends (sixteen-year-old girls are the same the world over). Sumayah, on the other hand, said she'd love to go. We picked an Italian restaurant for dinner. Little did I know what would happen next.

Upon entering the restaurant, the maitre d' instantly recognized Sumayah. (She later told me that he must have recognized her because she'd begged for food many times at the restaurant.) He glanced in my direction as if something about this situation wasn't right. I quickly pulled him aside and told him I was just trying to help Sumayah. He grasped my sincerity and decided everything was all right. Shortly after that, he rose to the occasion in a way that I have rarely seen in my life.

He took Sumayah by the arm and, treating her like Cinderella at the ball, said, "Madame, let me escort you to your table." He pulled out her chair, placed the napkin on her lap, and began one of the most beautiful series of gestures I have ever seen. Throughout the meal, he paid great attention to her and kept pouring water over his right arm, even though I noticed no one else got this kind of treatment. (I think the bill was $40. I tipped him $50—and he deserved every cent.)

Shortly after we sat down and ordered bread and some soda, Sumayah looked around with contentment. She smiled and said, "Bob, this is so nice. We're just sitting here, eating and talking. It's almost like we're human beings."

It's almost like we're human beings. I almost fell off my chair hearing that last sentence. Sumayah had lived for so long on the streets that I think both consciously and unconsciously, she had lost a great deal of her humanity. Struggling every day for survival can do that to a person. Eating and relaxing, things we often take for granted, helped restore a sense of humanity that was very real for her.

Since that night, I have often thought of that experience and the remarkable words *it's almost like we're human beings.*

For people who live on the edge of society and are forced to survive on the streets, they often feel more like animals than humans. Life on the street strips them of their dignity in a way that cuts to the core of their being. Like Sumayah, they feel less than fully human.

Sumayah taught me an incredible lesson on that unforgettable night. She not only felt more human but she made me feel that way too.

It is a gift I will never be able to repay.

4. Faith to Move Mountains

One of the most memorable aspects of this project has been meeting people who are doing heroic things for orphaned children, often with very few resources. People are taking in children in their neighborhoods, opening up small shelters in their backyards, and generally doing a lot with very little. But in my experience, one such person stands above them all.

Zodwa Mqadi was an HIV/AIDS counselor in Durban, a seaside South African city. Overwhelmed by the number of clients who died from HIV, Zodwa began caring for their orphaned children and opened the Agape Child Care Center in 1996. Shortly after, she faced enormous community pressure to leave the community because AIDS was misunderstood and no one wanted the children living near them. Zodwa stood her ground and refused to move. It was this kind of advocacy that marked her life.

When a fire destroyed most of the center in January 2005, the forty children moved into an old shipping container on the property. A shipping container looks similar to the trailer on a semitruck. It is simply a big steel box. The container was a less than adequate place for children to live, but Zodwa kept the kids together and dreamed of rebuilding.

In April of 2005, I visited Agape after hearing about Zodwa through a friend. At this point in our history, I was still looking for property for Open Arms and exploring the various approaches to the orphaned problem. I stayed at Agape for two days.

Seeing the situation at Agape was heartrending. Here were forty kids living in a shipping container. Zodwa didn't have a lot of connections to the outside world, so funding was a serious problem. She relied on local people to help with donations of money, food, or clothing. But it was apparent to me that she needed help and needed it badly. Her biggest dream was to rebuild the home and partner with people like us to secure funding from overseas. We talked about that possibility, and with forty kids right in front of me, it seemed like maybe this was God placing a project right in our lap. Most importantly, it was hard not to be incredibly inspired by the work that Zodwa had done.

When I left Zodwa, I gave her about $1,000 to keep going and told her I would be back in touch.

When I got back to the States, I discussed the situation at Agape with Sallie. We thought hard about partnering with Zodwa and building a new facility for them. But after much reflection and prayer, we concluded that we had a different vision for Open Arms. It was a very tough decision.

The call to Zodwa to tell her this news was not easy. I told her we had a vision of what we wanted Open Arms to be, and that even though we were moved by her plight, we were going to look elsewhere to get started.

"Don't worry about it, Bob," Zodwa told me over the phone. "I know God has planted a dream in your heart, and you should follow it. Don't worry, God will send us someone to help. I just know he will."

Being a churchgoing person, I was inspired by Zodwa's faith and her incredible tenacity in the face of a really bad situation. Cynically, it would have been very easy to dismiss her faith as naïve and unrealistic. She had no connections, no marketing, and no money.

But having witnessed what Zodwa had done for forty children with absolutely nothing but good intentions, I too prayed that someone would come along to help.

About four months later, I was on an airplane reading the *New York Times* when I read this headline: "African Orphans Give Their All, in Song, for New Home." Upon reading the article, I was astounded to learn that the talented pop singer Alicia Keys had come across the children's story and decided to help them! Alicia and some other people flew six of the children to New York to sing at a benefit concert, and funds were raised for a new home.

Since that time, the Agape Children's Choir has performed with Bono and Alicia Keys, and in venues in London and New York. There is even a documentary movie about them called *We Are Together*.

In the good book, Jesus says, "If you have faith the size of a mustard seed, you will say to this mountain 'move from here to there' and it will move. Nothing will be impossible for you." Zodwa proved that to be true right before my eyes. I will never forget her saying, "Don't worry, God will send us someone." And then he did!

Zodwa Mqadi died in 2010. If I have ever met a person who went straight to heaven on the fastest elevator, it was Zodwa. I hope that she will put in a good word for me. She had the faith to move mountains, and she actually did.

There is nothing as powerful as people who align their lives with God's plan for them. They don't need a detailed business plan but a calling and unshakable faith that God will be with them. Zodwa had both of the latter, and the results were utterly remarkable.

5. God in Khayelitsha

South Africa is full of areas called *townships* that often consist of substandard housing and a general lack of everything in the way of creature comforts. There is usually no indoor plumbing, no electricity, open sewers, and shacks made out of wood and corrugated tin or whatever anyone can find to make a "house."

I have been in many of these townships on my trips to the country. Almost all of the children at Open Arms come from such areas. Some of the larger townships have hundreds of thousands of people living in them.

On an early trip to Cape Town, I decided to visit a children's home in the middle of Khayelitsha, one of the largest townships in the country. Khayelitsha means "new home" in the Xhosa language, and it was established as place to put black people in a segregated area under the rule of Apartheid. Today, it is estimated that 400,000 people live in Khayelitsha, most of them in shacks.

As I drove myself to the children's home in the township, I was astounded by the number of shacks and people living in absolute squalor. I had seen poverty like this in Mexico, but not on the scale found in Khayelitsha. It was a mass of suffering humanity like I had never seen before.

Just prior to arriving at my destination, I had a certain feeling come over me, and I was absolutely sure of its truth. I am not sure why it came to me, because I had not been thinking about the topic when it entered my brain. But I knew it was right. The tears in my eyes only confirmed it.

For some reason, driving through square miles of shacks made me absolutely convinced that if God was to come to the earth today in the form of a human being, that person would be born in Khayelitsha. In a flash of insight, I was absolutely sure that if God was to send Jesus to us again, he would be born in this place. It was one of the most memorable insights I have ever had. You can doubt its veracity and question it on some theological basis, but I certainly didn't. And I still don't.

Reflecting on this message for weeks afterward, I came to realize why I was delivered such a stark message. The historical Jesus came from poor parents, was born in a stable, had no money and no discernible future, and was on the move all the time. People of privilege and power scoffed at him and ended up putting him to death because they believed him to be a rather dangerous fellow. He challenged the status quo and was killed for it.

On many levels, people who are born in Khayelitsha face the same obstacles. They have no privilege, power, or money and often face a very bleak future full of all sorts of suffering. People who live there often die for things like not having a few bucks to buy antibiotics or not having funds to pay for a needed surgery.

I'm not sure if God will come back to earth in the form of a human being again. That's his business, not mine. But if he does, I would expect him or her to be born in a place like Khayelitsha. No one would expect it, and I've come to learn that's where God usually comes from.

6. Motivation

Several years ago, I toured a place called Duncan Village, a large township that is about an hour's drive from Open Arms. I walked among the shacks and smelled the odor created by open sewers. As always, it was very humbling to go into a place where our brothers and sisters live in such squalor.

As my tour guide and friend Joyce and I walked down a path, we came across a lady standing out in front of her shack. Seeing how thin she was, it was very apparent that she had AIDS. Some people call the disease "slim" because of its effects on sufferers at the end of their lives. Joyce stopped to talk to the woman and offer her some emotional support.

During their conversation in Xhosa, I walked over to the woman's shack and looked inside. There, on a mattress on the dirt floor, lay a beautiful infant girl. She was asleep and looked angelic, like sleeping children often do.

Knowing that her mother was in such poor health, I instinctively wanted to pick up the child and take her to Open Arms. I knew she was in a very vulnerable situation, and I also knew it wouldn't be long until she became an orphan.

At Open Arms, however, our children come to us through the court system. We cannot go out into the community and take children in on our own. So I bent down, knocked a few flies off of the child, and put my hand on her forehead. And then I did what I usually do in such circumstances: I prayed. I asked God to take her into his arms and to alleviate the suffering that she was sure to face. And then, as I stood up, for some reason I took her photo. I'm not sure why I did this, but I can only surmise that I didn't want to forget two things: first, what she looked like, and second, that she represented to me why Open Arms Home for Children exists. When I got home, I filed my photos on the computer and went on with my life.

Twelve months later, I was back touring Duncan Village with two of our board members, Jeff Towery and Dave Horan. Like all of our board members, Dave and Jeff are tremendously committed to this cause and are frequent visitors to our campus. We were touring Duncan Village because I wanted them to see the conditions that our children come from.

Like the year before, Joyce, a community activist, was our tour guide. As we turned down one path after another, suddenly we found ourselves in the same location where I had seen the skinny woman standing in her yard. I immediately recognized the shack and turned to Joyce to ask her what had happened to the woman and her child.

She turned to me and said, "They didn't make it. They both died of AIDS." I almost fell down, and that's not an exaggeration.

"They *both* died?" I asked.

"Yes, they both passed from AIDS," she said.

I could not believe my ears. Standing outside that shack the year before, I had assumed the woman would pass away, but her daughter looked so healthy. I had no idea that the beautiful child in the tiny shack was HIV positive. If I had followed my instincts, I could have saved her life!

For the rest of day, I was in a fog. I couldn't believe that the girl I had prayed for was gone. I couldn't believe that she died of a disease that is eminently treatable. I couldn't believe that we live in a world where things like this happen.

I have looked at that girl's photo countless times since that day. I have no idea why she died. I have lots of questions and very few answers. But that is what life is like at the margins of humanity. The poor and suffering always have more questions than answers. The rich and strong, by contrast, always have far more answers than questions.

Today, I know that there is a child who is sleeping on a dirt floor who will die unless the rest of us do something about it. You can call that a stretch, but I don't think it's a stretch at all. It's the truth.

Sometimes, when I get tired of writing thank you notes or raising funds for Open Arms, I just have to look at the photo of that child and suddenly I'm not tired anymore. I know we have to carry on because I'm 100 percent sure that there is another child just like her who will soon need a home and a lot of love.

Looking at the photo of the beautiful girl, I still have a lot of questions. But I am sure of one thing: God did indeed answer the prayer I prayed with my hand on her head. He did take her in his arms. It was just in a way that I could never have expected and still cannot fully understand.

7. The Rocking Chair

About three months after our first trip to South Africa, I was on a plane returning to launch the investigatory phase of whether we should start this ministry. Prior to the trip, I was excited and nervous about traveling by myself to South Africa to continue looking at this problem and deciding whether our family could do something about it.

But about twenty minutes into the first leg of the journey, a flight from Phoenix to Minneapolis, I became paralyzed with fear. *What am I doing?* I asked myself. Here I was a financial advisor with a large family flying on a plane to Africa to start the process of opening an orphanage. I thought to myself, *I must be absolutely nuts. What kind of person does this with no experience and no real plan?* I rarely get filled with fear, but there I was, looking out the window of an airplane and wondering if a psychiatrist was on board to certify that I had lost my mind.

I do a lot of reading, and often in times of indecision, panic, or despair, I turn to books to try to find insight. Not knowing how to deal with my fear, I opened a book of quotations that I had brought along. I often find wisdom in quotations, and so instinctively I opened the book.

The first quote I read was from Mother Teresa. It was exactly what I needed to read. Apparently, when she was in her mid-eighties and suffering from poor health, a reporter asked Mother Teresa if she had plans to retire. She simply responded, "How can I sit in my rocking chair when the house is on fire?"

Right away, I felt at peace reading that quote. I suddenly felt that I was on the right plane at the right time hearing the right call. After all, after seeing so much suffering on our family trip, how could we sit in our rocking chairs when the house was indeed on fire?

Many times on this wonderful journey with Open Arms, the right word of encouragement has come along at exactly the right time, or a big donation comes in just when it is needed, or a person offers to help when precisely that kind of help is critical to our mission.

The Swiss psychiatrist Carl Jung called this phenomenon "synchronicity," or the experience of "meaningful coincidence." Based on my experience with Open Arms, I believe in the phenomenon, but I don't think it's merely coincidence. I choose to believe that it is Providence—God sending us support for his children. Jesus said, "All things are possible." So then I ask, what is left out? Absolutely nothing.

Since we started Open Arms, so many seemingly unrelated events have occurred to move this project along, including the Mother Teresa quote coming at exactly the right time.

Since reading that quote, I have never looked back. The house is indeed on fire, and the rocking chair seems like no place to sit.

Postscript: Now, several years after reading this quote from Mother Teresa, I can honestly say that I cannot find it recorded anywhere! I have searched my three books on Mother Teresa, a few quotation books that I own, and the internet as well. I can find no record of Mother Teresa ever saying such a thing, even though I know that I read it and remember wiping tears away after I came across it on the plane. Many years later now, I am not sure what to make of this.

There is a story about Mother Teresa that might shed some light here. According to the book Blessed Mother Teresa *by T.T. Mundakel, Mother once needed additional space for her ministry in Calcutta. A man came to her door and told her about a place that might be for sale that was appropriate for her work. The man led her to the owner of the building in question, and Mother Teresa asked him if he was willing to sell. The owner of the building was flabbergasted by the question, as he told Mother Teresa that he had not told anyone about his intention to sell except his wife. When Mother Teresa turned around, the man who had accompanied her to the building was gone. This was only one of many seemingly miraculous events that occurred during Mother Teresa's lifetime.*

Honestly, I cannot prove that Mother Teresa ever uttered the words "How can I sit in my rocking chair while the house is on fire?" But I am nonetheless convinced that I did read those words on a plane in early 2005, and they emboldened this project. Perhaps this was Mother Teresa's intervention or God's, but the message was very real to me, and it still is.

8. The Song

I often read spiritual or self-help books that describe life as a journey. I understand this because all of us, regardless of our station in life, travel on a journey from birth to death. We were all born, and given the fact that the mortality rate of human beings is still 100 percent, we all will meet death sooner or later. Everyone's journey contains these two distinct moments—one of embarkation and one of departure.

In between those two dates, everyone has a chance to do one thing: sing a song with their lives. I like to think of life that way. Our song—really The Song—can be loud, soft, depressing, fun, sad, happy, hard to listen to, or maybe even inspiring.

Here are the ten rules for The Song:

1. You only get to sing one song. It can have many verses, but you only get to sing one song. There are no dress rehearsals and there are no do-overs.
2. Others are encouraged to sing along with you, but in the end, your song is ultimately a solo and must remain so.
3. In the history of the world, the song you sing has never been heard before.

4. After you are gone, your song will never, ever be heard again. Never.

5. If you sing your song properly, it will attract others to listen to it. Properly sung, your song will most definitely become part of the song others will sing.

6. If you sing someone else's song, it will sound bad and others will not want to listen to it. The very best song you can sing is the one that is meant for you, and only you can determine what that is. If you accept external advice on your song, it will only deaden the lyrics and ruin the melody.

7. To make the most powerful song possible, you must believe in the song with all your heart. Completely authentic songs sung with 100 percent conviction are always the very best songs that are sung. The more you believe in your song, the more others will believe in it too.

8. Your song always has the ability to save others, and if you listen to others' songs, their songs have the ability to save you too.

9. You will hear your song sung back to you throughout your life. If you sing with joy, you will hear joyful songs. If you sing with sadness, you will hear sad songs. The song you sing will always come back to you just as you sing it.

10. Your very best song will be sung with your own voice and a melody written by God. Trying to figure out the tune and lyrics will be puzzling and even obscure at times. But there is a song waiting to be sung, and your very best song will always have God writing the music.

These are the ten laws of The Song. They cannot be changed, and they apply to every one of us.

9. Do It Now

Both of my parents died suddenly and without warning. My mother died in a car accident at age fifty-three, and my dad died at age sixty-six in his sleep. Neither of them had any warning that their lives were ending, nor did we get to exchange final goodbyes. I was a young adult when they passed away.

I wish with all my heart that my parents would have lived longer. I wish that they had the chance to get to know my wife better and to see their grandkids grow up. I wish they could visit Open Arms and see the joy of the children who live there.

That won't happen. But their early deaths did teach me a valuable lesson: if you want to do something with your life, don't wait until later. Later may never come.

When we thought about starting Open Arms, our own children were coming up on college. That is not a good time to do anything but start eating macaroni and cheese to save for tuition, room, and board. At the time we started this project, we had a mortgage, credit card bills, and the same financial concerns that most of us share. Financially, it was not a good time to start Open Arms.

However, having witnessed how quickly life goes and how quickly it can end, we knew we simply could not wait for a better time to start this project. For the orphaned children who were

21

suffering in silence without parents, they couldn't wait either. They needed homes.

One of the strangest things about death is that it contains great lessons for life. And one of the most important lessons from death is the urgency it creates to embark on a dream when it's possible and not when it's best.

We don't wait for all the traffic signals to turn green to drive the car out of the driveway. We don't wait for our financial goals to be completed before we have children of our own.

There is no time like now. We should never delay what we can do now in exchange for the possibility of never doing it later.

10. Thanks, Dad

We have a boy at Open Arms named Yanga who lost his parents at an early age. He was placed with a foster family for three or four years, and then his foster father died. We're not sure if Yanga ever knew his biological parents, but he certainly knew his foster father and loved him dearly. It was after his foster father died that he was placed at Open Arms.

Yanga has his share of challenges. He was born with fetal alcohol syndrome and is profoundly affected by it. At age eleven, he still has trouble reading, and school-based learning is very difficult for him. But Yanga has a good heart and is naturally compassionate. A visitor who was once having a very rough day because of illness still gets teary-eyed about how Yanga consoled her in the most tender way. Maybe children who suffer like Yanga just naturally know when some is feeling bad. It seems that way.

Every Friday at Open Arms, we have a therapist who comes to help the children deal with the many emotions they feel. Her name is Jeanien Marx, and she is a wonderful member of the Open Arms family. Jeanien cares deeply about the children, and we are blessed to have her with us.

One Friday, Jeanien asked Yanga to write down what he was feeling that day. Despite his very limited writing skills, Yanga wrote the following to his late foster dad: "I love you Dad and you love me too. Thank you for putting me at Open Arms."

When I saw those words written by Yanga, I cried a little bit myself. The man that Yanga considered his dad—his foster father—had nothing to do with him coming to Open Arms. That was decided after his death. But of course, Yanga believed it, and that was the most important thing. After all, why shouldn't a child believe that their parents are looking out for them? We all want to believe that.

I am not sure what the future will hold for Yanga. It may be difficult for him to finish school or hold a job. Regardless of his future, I know we will be there for him every step of the way. After all, he's depending on us—just like he depended on his foster father.

Open Arms Home for Children sits in a position of great responsibility and awesome privilege. Every day we try to earn the love and trust that the children give us so freely.

"Thank you for putting me at Open Arms," wrote Yanga. I pray to God that we live up to that. To me, it is the highest compliment we have received and reflects the great responsibility we carry for Yanga and all the little human beings who come to our doors.

11. A Letter from Bobo, Spring 2013

Twice a year, Open Arms Home for Children publishes a newsletter called "Open Arms News." We started doing this in 2009 in order to give our donors an update on our children and developments at the home. The first article in the newsletter is entitled "A Letter from Bobo." The children at Open Arms call me "Bobo" because it is easier for them to say than "Bob." Appropriately, it serves as the name for the cover article, and I am happy to share some of those letters throughout this book. This one appeared in the Spring 2013 edition of Open Arms News.

On Tuesday, March 12, I went to my job as a financial advisor in Sun City, Arizona. On that day, the Dow Jones average reached a new record high and investors celebrated the eighth straight day of a new stock market high. This was good news for sure.

That same day, I received an email from Open Arms stating that two month-old twin boys were in need of a home. Their father was dying of AIDS and had been unable to work for months. Their HIV-positive mother, broke and sick herself, was trying to care for two infants without food or money. On top of that, she knew that the only way she could feed them—breastfeeding—would risk transmitting the HIV virus to her boys.

Under unbearable pressure to feed her hungry sons, the mother knew that she had to do something. She was aware of Open Arms because a family member's child had been placed with many years before.

She did what most of us would find unthinkable: she called Open Arms and asked us to take her sons away.

Such situations are not rare at Open Arms, and they simply break my heart. On March 12, on one side of the globe, investors rejoiced that their investments were bringing them new wealth. On the other side of the planet, a sick and desperately poor mother could not feed her sons because she had no money and suffers from a disease that turns breastfeeding into a dangerous game of Russian roulette. How do things like this happen?

I'm not sure I'll ever have the answer to that question. But I do know one thing: on March 12, 2013, thanks to you, those boys had a place to go where they were fed, bathed, and held in loving arms. They were welcomed into a new family that you, our donors, make possible.

As I write this, I am filled with unspeakable gratitude for the home that you make possible at Open Arms. But on March 12, my gratitude was dwarfed by the thankfulness of that poor mother. While I thank you from my heart, she thanks you from the depths of her soul.

We are privileged to be engaged in this work with you.

12. Hope

On a trip to the Duncan Village township, I once saw a shack made of corrugated tin. It had rocks on the roof to keep it from blowing off in the wind. It was similar to every one of the thousands of shacks I saw that day—except for one thing.

Just outside the door of the shack, the person who lived there had planted five or six flowers in the dirt. They were impatiens, the same flowers we have always planted at our house.

There, growing in the midst of a great deal of suffering, were flowers planted by someone who had not lost hope. In the middle of a neighborhood teeming with sewage and without electricity or running water, the resident of the ramshackle shack had made a stand and planted some flowers. It spoke to me of human dignity in a very profound way.

In the midst of the darkness of a slum, those flowers represented a ray of light. I am sure the neighbors appreciated the sight of bright flowers just as much as the homeowner did. And so did this visitor from overseas.

Hope is the most precious of commodities. It separates human beings from other animals. And most beautifully, it causes people to plant flowers in a place where no flowers should be.

13. The Only Bible Some People Will Ever Read

Fr. Billy Barnes is a South African Catholic priest who has become a good friend over the years. He is a lifelong friend of some clients of mine who met him when he toured the United States several decades ago. He has given more than fifty years of service to God's people, and he is as quick with a joke as he is with a scripture quote. Needless to say, he's my kind of guy!

I usually meet Fr. Barnes for lunch on every trip to South Africa. He lives about an hour's drive from Open Arms, and it is a delight to be his friend. He has done a lot for the home by mobilizing locals to help in many ways. Sweaters have been knitted, shoes collected, and prayers offered all because of Billy Barnes's advocacy of Open Arms.

I have only attended regular Sunday mass at Fr. Barnes' church in East London once. But he gave a sermon that I won't soon forget.

On that particular morning, Fr. Barnes talked about two men that lived next door to each other for years. One was a Christian, the other an atheist. He said both men lived similar lives. They both worked hard and stayed pretty much to themselves, and there wasn't anything particularly noteworthy about either man. The only major difference was that one went to church every Sunday, while the other did not.

One day, the Christian decided to sneak over to the front porch of his neighbor to leave a Bible outside the door. About an hour later, the Christian received a knock on the door. The atheist stood there and simply said, "I saw you leave the Bible outside my front door. If you want to retrieve it, you can go to the alley. You'll find it on top of my garbage cans."

"Don't you want to read it?" said the Christian.

"No," said the atheist, "I don't need to. I have watched you live your life for more than twenty years, and if your life is based on that book, I don't see that it's worth reading. The Bible hasn't inspired you to do anything differently than me, and I'm *not* a believer. I don't need to read a book like that."

The point of Fr. Barnes sermon was that the only Bible that some people will ever read is our lives. He challenged us to think about that. What do our lives say about the book we profess to believe? What do our lives say to the nonbeliever?

It was a wonderful sermon and certainly captured the truth. After all, if the actions of our lives don't reflect the good news of the gospel, then what kind of good news is it?

An English churchman named Thomas Fuller once wrote, "He does not believe who does not live according to his belief." Fr. Barnes brought that point home and then some.

14. Perspective

....

People frequently ask me how my experiences in Africa have changed my life. To be honest, that can be as hard to answer as figuring out the impact our parents had on us. We know we have been impacted profoundly, but it's hard to pin down a list of five or ten things.

But I do know this: I used to get upset when the car didn't start or the computer didn't work. I don't anymore. I have a car and a computer.

I used to get upset when the stubborn old toilet got clogged at our house. I don't anymore. I have a toilet.

I used to be mildly irritated by having to change our drinking water filters once a year at our home. I don't anymore. I have clean drinking water.

I used to get irritated by the twenty-minute wait at the local pharmacy. That doesn't bother me anymore. I have access to cheap and effective medicine.

I used to get mad at having to commute to work in bad traffic. I don't anymore. I have a job.

There is a famous saying that goes, "I lamented that I had no shoes until I met the man with no feet." I have met that guy.

Come to think of it, I don't really care much about my shoes anymore either.

15. A Death in the Family

Nothing strikes at the core of your being like a death in the family. There is no experience in life like losing a close loved one. It is part of the human experience, but its commonality doesn't make it anything less than the most painful experience most of us ever have.

In the spring of 2011, Open Arms received two children from the hospital. The twin sisters, Sisana and Buiswa, had been born very underweight to a young mother. They needed a home, and we were happy to provide it.

At Open Arms, nothing generates a buzz around the campus like when we take in an infant. Our mamas hover over the new child just like new mothers, and our older children flock to the nursery to hold and play with the baby. This excitement is no different at Open Arms than it is in households the world over. New life is celebrated and welcomed.

Upon coming to Open Arms, the two sisters were quite obviously in poor health. They were tiny, weighing less than five pounds each, and they suffered from frequent colds and respiratory problems. We made frequent visits to the local clinic to stay on top of their fragile health.

One of the sisters, Sisana, had particular problems. She failed to put on weight and just never got going. Doctors call this "failure to thrive," and that term described Sisana. She just did not make the progress that her sister was making, even though that was slow too.

During her twelfth week of life, it was clear that Sisana was particularly congested. We took her to the doctor every day, and when she didn't improve, we admitted her to the hospital in East London. Mama Potso, one of our staff members, stayed with her 24/7.

On the second day of her hospital stay, little Sisana began to fight for her life. She struggled to breathe, and the doctors did their best to keep her alive. However, the fight was in vain. On her second night at the hospital, she left this world and entered another.

There is simply no preparation for an event like this. There is no explanation for it either. The entire Open Arms family on both sides of the Atlantic cried for a lost sister. Some people are given eighty years to live; Sisana was given exactly eighty days.

At Open Arms, we still grieve for Sisana. There is no getting over that. We don't know why she left us far too soon. We don't know why she didn't survive like her sister, who remains with us and often gets hugged just a little tighter than the other kids for reasons that are far too obvious.

But despite our questions, we do know this: for her short time on earth, Sisana thought the world was a pretty good place. She knew the love of family, the feeling of kisses on the forehead, and the hugs of adults and children alike. She knew that she was loved, and she knew that she had a family.

Even today, more than three years later, that is the only solace we can take for a loved one that left us far too soon.

After she died, we decided to have a star named for Sisana. Quite appropriately, it is located in the constellation of Gemini, the twin. It seemed appropriate to name a star after this little girl who all touched our hearts and still causes tears to flow.

To astronomers, the star "Sisana" can be found in Gemini with the coordinates of RA6h59m5.00s. To members of the Open Arms family, the star is found in our hearts. It remains the only star that we can see without looking up.

16. A Meaningful Prayer

Quite often, I attend weekday morning mass at my parish of St. John Vianney in Goodyear, Arizona. The mass starts at six-thirty a.m. every weekday, and it is a good way to start my day before going to work.

During the mass, there is a time when the congregation is asked to offer up prayers of intention to God. These often range from prayers for sick relatives to prayers for peace or for the protection of our troops overseas. The prayers are offered up with great sincerity, and the congregation answers by saying "Lord, hear our prayer."

Without exception, one elderly man offers up a prayer that I find exceptionally moving. It always reminds me of the work that we do at Open Arms.

At the appointed time, the man simply says "For those who have no one to pray for them." The prayer only has ten words, but I find it one of the most moving and meaningful prayers I have ever heard.

The essence of the work of Open Arms is to serve children who are all alone in the world. Prior to coming to our doors, they have no one to care for them and no one to pray for them.

As Christians, we are called to be Christ's for one another. And watching Jesus's example, it is clear that he had a special concern for those who had no one to pray for them: lepers, the blind and lame, the poor, prostitutes, and children. Despite the fact that these people were at the bottom of society's totem pole, Christ consistently gave them special attention and extra priority.

"For those who have no one to pray for them." The prayer reminds us of the countless people who suffer every day in loneliness and obscurity. More importantly, it begs the question: What are we going to do about it?

17. A Great Truth

....

Warren Zevon was a singer and songwriter who produced such hits as "Werewolves of London" and "Poor, Poor Pitiful Me." He was not a mainstream rock star but drew critical acclaim for his music and his dark, often humorous lyrics. Music giants such as Bob Dylan, Bruce Springsteen, Jackson Browne, and Don Henley were among many friends who were inspired by his work. Perhaps his biggest fan was David Letterman, who had him as a guest on *Late Show with David Letterman* many times. In addition, Zevon often filled in for band leader Paul Shaffer on Letterman's show when Paul was on vacation. As a result of their time together, Warren and Dave became good friends.

On Wednesday, October 30, 2002, Letterman afforded Zevon a rare honor: he made him the only guest on his hour-long show. This was highly unusual, but there was a good reason for the honor: just a month prior to the show, Zevon had been diagnosed with inoperable lung cancer that had spread throughout his body. He had very little time to live—the doctors gave him three months—and Letterman wanted to honor his good friend with a full show focusing on Warren Zevon the man, the artist, and most of all, the good friend.

On the show, Letterman interviewed Zevon, and they talked openly about the diagnosis, Zevon's outlook on things, and on the impending end they both knew would come. During the interview, which clearly was a conversation among friends, Letterman asked Zevon a question that was a bit unusual for a funny late-night talk show. The question simply was this: "From your perspective now, do you know something about life and death that maybe I don't know now?"

Zevon paused for a second and answered, "Not unless I know how much you're supposed to *enjoy every sandwich*." There was a momentary silence in the theater. It was the kind of silence that occurs whenever a simple but profound truth has been spoken.

Within a year, Warren Zevon was dead. But before he died, he wrote, sang, and produced his last album, *The Wind*, and witnessed the birth of his twin grandsons. Many of his friends helped contribute to the making of the last album as a way to spend time with a man who meant so much to them. For that album, Zevon won two Grammy awards. They were awarded after his death.

Due to magic of the internet, it is easy to watch this episode of *Late Show with David Letterman* online. I would recommend it. But more critically, I think it's far more important that we heed the words of a man who was staring death in the face and offered us timeless advice: "Enjoy every sandwich."

I'm not sure I've ever heard more profound words ever come out of my TV.

Jesus said, "Take no thought of the morrow." Zevon made it even more simple. "Enjoy every sandwich."

Let us live out his heartfelt advice while we can.

18. Long International Flights

One of the realities of running an organization that is exactly 10,147 miles from my front door in Arizona is that it requires a lot of time sitting in an airplane. Three times each year, I usually travel on Delta Airlines to South Africa. This route requires a four-hour flight to Atlanta, a sixteen-hour nonstop leg to Johannesburg, a ninety-minute domestic flight to East London, and a one-hour car ride to Open Arms. If there is one thing I could change about Open Arms, it would be the distance from my home. Most of the time, Brazil or Argentina look close on a map compared to the journey to the tiny hamlet of Komga, South Africa. But barring a massive shift of the earth's tectonic plates in the next few decades, the distance will remain.

I have developed ten rules for traveling on grueling international flights. This is by no means a comprehensive list but rather time-tested, battle-proven suggestions to endure long bouts in a coach seat.

1. Always think good thoughts about the trip prior to embarkation. Positive thoughts about luggage, the potential size of the person next to you, flight delays (no such thing), crying babies, and the general use of deodorant by fellow

travelers is required. Negative emotions in any of these areas will undoubtedly land you in a middle seat in row sixty-three as your plane sits for three hours on the tarmac with a mechanical problem while your bags head in the opposite direction to Detroit. Stay positive or any number of less-than-positive events will happen.

2. If you have a sensitive stomach (I do), or even if you don't, never try the mango-flavored couscous or the unidentifiable salad product on the plane, especially in the first hour of a sixteen-hour flight. With 268 passengers on board, the lines for a bathroom in a Boeing 777 can get long, and reading *War and Peace* while cramping in the john is not encouraged.

3. Seat location is everything. Nirvana on the Johannesburg flight for a passenger in coach is row 29. There is unlimited legroom, and you are the first coach passenger off the plane, so you can get through South African immigration quicker. Seats B, C, F, or G in row 44 are next on the priority list because they also provide unlimited legroom. If I don't have seats in these two rows, all blood exits my legs ninety minutes into the flight, and I spend the next fifteen hours thinking positive thoughts about how wonderful it is to live *without* deep vein thrombosis (see rule #1). A website called seatguru.com shows the best and worst seats on every scheduled airline flight in the world. I use it religiously, if only to convince myself that my middle seat is a lot better than the guy who is sitting on the aisle just outside of the bathroom after couscous is served.

4. When entering the plane on a transatlantic flight, never ever look to the left. This will be the worst thing that you can do for yourself. The area to the left is reserved for people who you will learn to dislike quickly. Unlike you, they will have unlimited drinks, sleep on a flat bed, enjoy four or five ice cream sundaes on the trip, and will arrive rested,

drunk, and able to move their lower extremities. If you do look to the left on boarding, you will spend the next sixteen hours wondering how you can sell a family member or two to scrape together the ten grand required for first class on your next trip.

5. In the year prior to your departure, do not watch movies in the theater, on Netflix, or anywhere. One of the great advances of international travel in the last ten years is the development of a personal entertainment system for passengers—even in coach. Usually, at least a couple of dozen movies are offered for viewing. If you are a movie buff back home, then chances will be good that the only movie you haven't seen on the flight is a Chinese documentary about cramped conditions for coach passengers on international flights. If you haven't been in a theater for at least a year, odds are good you will actually enjoy a movie for at least twenty minutes before the couscous takes hold. With a limited selection of movies to watch, novelty is critical to make the sixteen hours seem only like fifteen and a half.

6. Always wear a navy blue or black shirt. One of the most consistent realities of international flying is that just as you eat your first bite of food, the severe turbulence will begin. Since all food in coach has some sort of a sauce to mask its true taste, this means your shirt or blouse will have a stain at some point in the trip, usually right after takeoff on the first leg. Stains are much easier to hide on black or navy blue. God forbid you wear white and then have people chuckling at you for the next day and a half, knowing that you either haven't read this book (a big problem) or you belong to a cult that proudly displays a brown gravy stain as its unifying symbol.

7. If you are ever bumped off a plane in an interesting city, be prepared for a really poor experience. I have been bumped off of planes in places like Amsterdam, Paris, and Brussels.

This always happens on a night flight, meaning that they put you up overnight in the worst hotel in town; all the good ones are obviously booked. Only the Le Roach Parisian will have room for you, and it will offer you three hours of interrupted sleep before you head back to the airport for the five a.m. flight. Every five a.m. flight in the world is designed to give bumped passengers somewhere to go, because no sane traveler would actually schedule such a thing.

To make matters worse, the airline will give you a voucher for a late evening buffet meal at the hotel, and this voucher will allow you to tell people for the rest of your life that the worst food in the world is found in (insert city here). This is not the case, of course, but your voucher-provided meal is guaranteed to make you feel like a true authority. I especially recommend the foam cake for dessert. I think it's made by Owens-Corning.

If you get bumped off a flight in Akron or Yuma, you will be at a much nicer hotel with better food. Very few people travel to those places on purpose, meaning you will be bumped to one of the best places in town and begin to wonder why anyone ever goes to Paris.

8. Deodorant and antiperspirant. Only two things need be said here. The first: apply it liberally in five coats before you leave home. You will do yourself and other passengers a favor. Remember, you will not be showering for more than two days. The second: always bring one or two of those mini-deodorants in a little cellophane bag on board the airplane. You will find them handy to secretly drop on the seat of Johnny or Joan Stinkpits when they get up to deal with the couscous cramps or to wipe the gravy stain off their new white shirt. They may not get the hint, but you will entertain yourself for a few minutes on the flight as they look around for the culprit. It also gives you the

opportunity to be a hero to the next person they sit near on a sixteen-hour flight.

9. Bring one of those neck pillows on any international flight. This will ensure that you get to your destination with only severe neck pain. It is no coincidence that those pillows look like cervical collars. Not using one, however, is fully endorsed by your local chiropractor. It's your call.

10. Mango-flavored couscous is wonderful for irregularity. If they offer it just prior to landing at your final destination, ask the guy next to you if you can have his too. You can thank me later.

19. Shoes

In 2006, the *Daily Dispatch* newspaper in the nearby city of East London ran a story about two boys, ages three and nine, who were living on their own in a shack in a township. Their mother, too sick from HIV/AIDS to care for them, was in a hospital while they struggled to get by. The boys begged to stay alive and lived on their own. Such situations are common in AIDS-stricken sub-Saharan Africa, and they are called "child-headed households." I think that is the most antiseptic term we could give them. In plain English it means kids are on their own, they're begging to stay alive, and life absolutely sucks.

The two boys' names were Khanyisa, age nine, and Kwame, age three. They lived among shacks and went wherever anyone would take them in. Khanyisa was so traumatized by their situation that he stopped talking all together. He would not speak to anyone but looked after his brother as best he could and hoped for some relief.

That relief came after their story hit the newspaper and authorities intervened. The boys were taken by social workers to a local magistrate who assigned them to the only children's home in the area that had space, Open Arms. At the time, we had just opened our doors and had only two children calling us home.

The adjustment for Khanyisa and Kwame was not easy, but they were glad to have a warm bed and good food. Like many of our kids, they stored food under their beds the first few weeks. When you've been hungry to the depths of your being, you try to make sure that doesn't happen again. Eventually, they came to understand that they would get three meals a day and stopped storing food.

Because of his mom's poor health and poverty, Khanyisa had never been to school. He had always wanted to go but couldn't due to his circumstances. After about three weeks of living with us, we enrolled him in first grade.

I happened to be at Open Arms the night before Khanyisa's first day of school ever. Here he was, at age nine, finally going to first grade. He was considerably taller than the other kids he would be going to school with, but he couldn't have cared less. We bought him a uniform and some black leather shoes and prepared him for the big day. He was a bit nervous but even more excited. A dream was coming true for him.

When I tucked Khanyisa into bed the night before school started, he said in broken English "Bobo, shoes, Bobo, shoes." Not speaking his native Xhosa language, I just said "Ok, Khanyisa, please do whatever you need to do with your shoes." He then proceeded to break my heart.

Going across the bedroom, Khanyisa took his new black shoes and began to spit shine them for the next ten minutes. I tried to hide the tears but I just couldn't. Here was a young boy getting ready for the first day of formal education in his life, and he couldn't have been more proud or excited. For him, it was a dream come true to attend school, and he wanted to look his level best. The simple act of shining his black shoes proved the point in the most poignant way.

For those of us who often take schooling for granted, Khanyisa provided a stark reminder that for many children in the world, education is a privilege and not a right. As he shined his shoes with obvious delight, I felt privileged to witness such a heartwarming and life-affirming thing. I will go to my grave with that memory.

Khanyisa proved to me, as all of our children do, that from the darkest places come the brightest lights.

20. Under Starry Skies

There is nothing quite as breathtaking as looking up at the stars in an area where there are no city lights and very little pollution. Those conditions make watching the night sky at Open Arms incredibly rewarding.

I have been a lot of places in the world, and the night sky at Open Arms is probably the best vantage point I've ever had to take in the glory of the heavens. After the kids go to bed, I usually head out to our tennis court (a.k.a. bike riding arena because we've never played tennis there) to take in the inspiring light show.

Because of the awesome visibility, you can see lots of galaxies, every constellation you know (I know a whopping three), and a shooting star seems to come across the southern sky about every five minutes. A few years back, some board members and I watched a huge comet cross the sky from east to west. The incredible display took over thirty minutes to pass by, and it was the most fantastic cosmic display I've ever seen.

On my last few visits, I have used the time after dinner to lie on the hillside with the children to stargaze, talk about their lives, and play what I call "The Question Game." I used to play the game with my own children, and they loved it as much as the kids at Open Arms do.

We lie on the grass and look up at the heavens, and I ask questions on topics ranging from sports, history, and animals to what is bigger, what is smaller, who did what, etc. Children love to have their knowledge tested, and it's a great time to just relax and laugh.

Last night when we were playing the question game, I asked the kids, "Can you imagine if the stars of the sky only came out once per year?" I asked them what people would do if we only got to see the glory of God's heavens once every 365 days.

Very quickly, one of our boys answered, "Bobo, if that happened, we'd lie here just like this and play the question game."

When I heard that response, it was one of those moments in life when you know that you are in the right place at the right time and you're doing exactly what you're supposed to be doing. Those moments are rare, but we all have them. Elie Wiesel, in his famous book *Night*, described such moments as times when "question and answer become one." Regardless of what we call them, such grace-filled moments bring an inner peace that is hard to describe.

Every once in a while, God lets us know that despite our flaws and sins, He is still with us in a very real and tangible way. Last night was one of those nights. Lying under awesome stars with even more awesome children, the stars most certainly were lined up right.

21. Six Powerful Words

William Borden was born in 1887 into a very wealthy family in Chicago. His family owned Borden, the giant milk and dairy company. Quite candidly, Bill Borden was born with a silver spoon in his mouth, and even at his birth, it was fully expected that he would one day run the company bearing his name.

Upon graduating from high school, Bill's graduation gift from his parents was a round-the-world, year-long trip. Bill eagerly set off for Europe, Africa, and Asia and quickly discovered that not everyone in the world was as privileged as he was. Spurred on by his deep faith in Christ, Bill soon developed a calling to be a missionary. Quite shockingly, he decided to renounce his wealth for the sake of God and others. During his trip abroad, he wrote two simple words in his Bible: "No reserves." This meant that he would give his money away and keep none for himself. It also meant that he intended to be fully used up by God during his lifetime. There would be no gas left in the tank when he died.

After his year abroad, Bill enrolled at Yale University. The year was 1905. Borden quickly found Yale to be a very secular institution, so he decided to organize Bible study groups for students. Because of his charisma and utter dedication to his faith, by the time he was a senior, more than a thousand of Yale's 1,300 students were attending one of the Bible studies he organized. What's more, Borden also founded the Yale Hope Mission to serve homeless and destitute people in New Haven, Connecticut. He even bought the building that housed the mission. On nights and weekends, Borden could often be found at the Mission talking to people about Christ or just hearing their story or serving them a warm meal.

Upon graduating from Yale, Borden entered the seminary at Princeton in order to become a missionary. His father disagreed with his choice of careers and told him he would never again be welcome to work at the Borden Company. Shortly after this time, Bill Borden wrote two more words in his Bible: "No retreat." He was committed to following his heart and his faith no matter what the cost.

After graduating from seminary, Borden decided that he would go to work as a missionary among a Muslim population in Northern China. To do so, he needed to learn Arabic, so he stopped in Cairo to learn the language. After one month in Cairo, Borden tragically contracted cerebral meningitis and died at age twenty-five. Shortly before his death, he wrote two more words in his Bible: "no regrets."

William Borden left the great bulk of his estate to a missionary group called the China Inland Mission. This missionary group took the money and founded Borden Memorial Hospital in Langzou, China. The hospital still exists today and continues to bear his name. Although Borden never made it to China, his spirit and his money did, and a hospital bearing his name continues to operate more than one hundred years after his death.

William Borden was buried in the American Cemetery in Cairo, Egypt. The epitaph on his grave marker is among the most beautiful I have ever come across. It reads: "Apart from faith in Christ, *there is no explanation for such a life.*" [Emphasis is mine.]

William Borden's life should serve as a clarion call to Christians everywhere. We are called to surrender to Christ and his call in our lives—no matter what the cost. As William Borden showed us, that's not supposed to be a casual thing just reserved for Sundays or for our free time. It's supposed to be an all-the-time, lay-down-your-life kind of thing. This kind of commitment is not only hard to do but pretty damn inconvenient too.

William Borden gave everything he had to God: his time, his life, and his money. He was born into an incredibly wealthy family and decided to give it all up for God and others. And the headstone got it right: "Apart from faith in Christ, there is no explanation for such a life."

It's good to reflect on lives like Borden's. It certainly begs the questions: What is the best explanation for our lives? Could the same words be written on our headstone?

Perhaps the six handwritten words in Borden's personal Bible should serve as our best guide: "No reserves. No retreat. No regrets."

22. The End of the Road

In 2008, I walked 710 miles across South Africa to raise funds for more cottages at Open Arms. At the time, we were out of space to accept more children. While on the walk, I wrote a daily blog to keep our donors and friends informed of our progress. This was the entry from the final day of the walk.

A Long Walk for Children has ended! It has been an incredible journey and one that I'll never forget. John Ruskin once said that "the highest reward for a person's work is not what they get for it, but what they become by it." I am not sure what I've become through this experience, but as I come to the end of the walk and the daily blog entry, I am filled with two emotions: gratitude and a strengthened sense of commitment. I will expand upon these here.

Gratitude. This is the overwhelming emotion I have felt these past few days. I am grateful for so many things:

- That we made it 700 miles in safety in thirty days with no injuries or accidents.
- That our generous donors have helped us reach our fundraising goal of $250,000 (2 million rand).
- That so many friends and family provided constant encouragement along the way.

49

- That the Rotary Clubs of South Africa responded so magnificently, especially the East London Sunrise Club.
- That my employer and my clients supported this and allowed my six-week absence.
- That we will be able to expand our services to another forty to fifty children in the next few years.
- That our children and staff had a remarkable journey to Cape Town that they will never forget.
- That I will be able to return to my family in one piece!
- Lastly, that God has blessed this project in so many ways.

I want all of you reading this to know that none of this would have happened without you. When I write that this was a collective effort, I am making the understatement of the year! Everyone involved, including those of you who donated, those of you who prayed for us, and those who supported this in any way, should feel great about the impact that you are making on children's lives. On the blog, I have shared with you some of our children's stories. In so many ways, they are heartbreaking. But thanks to you, our kids now have love, hope, and opportunity in their lives. This is a great gift to our children and a source of tremendous joy for our donors and friends. Thank you from the bottom of my heart!

Commitment. As this journey ends, I know that the work is just beginning. There are so many children without homes and there is so much that we can do to expand this ministry. With every step I made, I knew that there would be more journeys ahead and much more work to do. That is both challenging and exciting. Now that the walk is finished, I feel that commitment even more strongly.

As many of you know, we called this "A Long Walk for Children" because the autobiography of Nelson Mandela is called "Long Walk to Freedom." I can in no way compare my journey to Mr. Mandela's lifetime of heroic action. A 700-mile walk does not mean anything compared to a lifetime of work to bring justice to 45 million people. However, at the end of his autobiography, Mr. Mandela ends by writing a paragraph that in many ways echoes my feelings today, and so I thought I'd share it with you:

> I have walked that long road to freedom. I have tried not to falter. I have made missteps along the way. But I have discovered the secret that after climbing a great hill, one only finds that there are many more hills to climb. I have taken a moment here to rest, to steal a view of the glorious vista that surrounds me, to look back on the distance I have come. But I can only rest for a moment, for with freedom come responsibilities, and I dare not linger, for my long walk is not yet ended.

And so I finish this blog the same way that I started it—with a photo of a child. This photo was taken of a child I came across in a township named Duncan Village in East London, South Africa. I was on a tour of the area and came across her sleeping on a mattress on a dirt floor in a tiny shack. I instantly wanted to take the child to Open Arms because she was certainly in a precarious situation. But we cannot take children without a court order, so I merely put my hand on her forehead, said a brief prayer for her, and took a photo because I did not want to forget the moment.

A year later, I was walking in the same area with some of our board members and came across the tiny shack. Not forgetting my experience a year earlier, I asked what had happened to that child and her mother. I was told: "They didn't make it. They both died of AIDS."

I think about that child often and did so many times on a journey across a beautiful land. I thought about how she died and whether she suffered greatly. I also think about what she might have become if we had reached her. A wife and a mother? A good friend? A person of faith? A source of inspiration to others? We'll never know.

But as I think about her now, I think about so many children like her, and I know that she did not die in vain. She is still with us in memory and still with us in the important work that we will carry on in the months and years ahead. Her journey is over, but ours continues with all the love and commitment we can give it.

May God bless you all. I look forward to continuing our work with you on the journey ahead. There are many more hills to climb, and so much is riding on the result.

Bob Solis
signing off on September 14, 2008

23. An Eye-Opener

One of the best concepts for bringing a family together is the family vacation. Sallie and I had our children young, so we didn't always have a lot of money to take our kids on a family vacation. Despite that, we always made it a priority to have one, and those trips are legendary in our family's collective memory. To this day, we cherish the time we spent together on those vacations.

At Open Arms, we want to create similar memories for our kids. Our operating budget cannot sustain a "family" vacation every year, but we do make it a priority to go every three years. In 2008, all of the children and staff went to Cape Town to help me finish my 700-mile walk across South Africa. In 2011 and 2014, we went on a three-day holiday to the seaside city of Durban.

On our first trip in 2008, it was remarkable to see the giddiness and excitement generated by a ten-hour bus trip to Cape Town. What I remember most is that our staff members were more excited than the children.

Imagine being fifty years old and eating in a restaurant for the first time in your life. That was Letta, our gardener. Imagine being nearly sixty years old and spending your first night in a hotel. That was Mariam, one of our caregivers. Imagine being Volia, forty-five, another caregiver, going to Robben Island to see the prison cell where her hero, Nelson Mandela, was imprisoned before helping her attain the freedom that she had been denied all of her life. It was a trip that included many firsts, but the most incredible ones were experienced by our staff.

For Sallie and me, the trip to Cape Town was one more reminder of how privileged we have been. On the first night at a hotel, one of our mamas asked us if there was an extra charge to take a shower. Someone else asked us if it was OK to turn on the TV. Several others were nearly in tears upon seeing the free breakfast buffet at the hotels. They had never lived in such luxury. Believe me, "all-you-can-eat" took on a new meaning that first breakfast. We'll never be invited back!

Such experiences are the benefit of travel. Travel allows people to share experiences they never thought they'd have. For our staff, that included staying in a hotel or eating in a restaurant for the first time in their lives and living in a way that most of us accept as the norm. For Sallie and me, the travel with the kids and staff reminded us of how blessed we have been and just how humbled we should be by those blessings.

Family vacations are important whether you have two kids in your family or fifty like we do in South Africa. And truth be told, it's often the "big kids," the adults, who have the most fun.

24. Life on the Edge

For people who live on the edge of life in poverty and pain, just about any day can bring sadness and the possibility of tragedy. When you live in life's shadow, the distance between today and tragedy is not very far. In the United States, tragedy is often kept at bay because of our nice houses, good health care or ample food. For example, it is very unlikely for me to encounter a neighbor dying of a disease that could have been successfully battled with fifty dollars to buy an antibiotic. For the poorest of the poor, such things can happen at almost any time, either in your own house or the one next door.

One time, I traveled with the children at Open Arms to a town named Butterworth to serve sandwiches to people who live near the town dump. The kids enthusiastically made fifty box lunches complete with bologna sandwiches, fruit, and chips. We also took along twenty beautiful quilts made by a group of ladies on St. Croix to give away to people in need of them—in other words, everyone we met at the dump.

On the thirty-minute drive, we came across a one car accident where a truck had just recently slammed into a rock wall on the side of the highway. The driver of the truck had obviously gone through the windshield and lay dead on the side of the road about two feet from where we drove past. Thankfully, the children did not see him lying there with his skull crushed in the back. But I saw it, and it shook me up. My mother died in a car accident, and I am always unnerved by such sights. It was a reminder not only of my mother but of the fragility of life on the way to serve people who know what fragility means in a way that I cannot.

Ten minutes after seeing this shocking sight, we arrived at the dump armed with box lunches and deep compassion for whoever we might see there. Because it was a Saturday and no garbage trucks were dumping, the usual foragers who look through the garbage for anything to eat or keep were not there. They had completed their work the day before. Instead, we just pulled into the dump, and people from the nearby shacks started coming out almost immediately. We have served food at the dump before, and it was obvious that the people recognized the Open Arms vans. People of all ages were soon all around us.

As in previous visits, our children presented the lunches they had prepared, and words of gratitude were exchanged. The blankets were also given out, instantly becoming the nicest possession in most of the recipients' households. Our good friends on St. Croix who make the quilts do a marvelous job of making them beautiful and one of a kind. In this case, they made them with great love specifically for people who live in the Butterworth dump. They knew the kids at Open Arms serve food there, and they wanted to help. Quite obviously, the quilts were accepted with great joy by people who not only need every bit of winter warmth they can find but anything that is clean and beautiful in their lives. I know that when the ladies on St. Croix get to heaven, they will be given quilts made out of gold—and they deserve them. They have lovingly made a quilt for every child at Open Arms since we opened our doors, and now that work has extended to a dump far from the beauty of St. Croix.

Because of the number of people who came running into the dump, the whole thing took no longer than fifteen minutes.

It is very humbling to do this kind of work. You know that you are just putting a tiny Band-Aid on terribly crushing poverty. After all, what are a bologna sandwich and a blanket to someone who lives in a shack? It's just a pleasant surprise on a Saturday afternoon, but chances are good the surprise will not be repeated for a good long time. The crushing poverty resumes as soon as the vans roll out.

Nevertheless, the kids at Open Arms like to carry on this work. They like to serve people in need, having usually lived in similar circumstances sometime in their past. They know from where they come and how blessed they are to have a warm bed, food, and lots of hugs each day. They have a natural compassion for people who don't have those things in their lives.

In the course of a few hours, we made a bunch of lunches, loaded up some blankets, saw a dead man on the side of the road, drove to a dump, and served people who need a lot more than a sandwich and a quilt. It was a stark reminder that the distance between highs and lows seems much closer in South Africa than it does in Phoenix. As the trip to the dump revealed once again, life on the margin is much different than anything I will ever know. It is much more confusing, sad, fragile, and dirty, and the distance between today and tragedy is often just outside the door of the shack where you live.

25. What You Do …

There are many passages in the Gospels where Jesus tells us that service is the true measure of a Christian. It is not judging the behavior of others—he rails against that repeatedly. It is not being successful at business—he warns us over and over that wealth is often a great obstacle to godliness. And it is not being religious in the eyes of the world—perhaps no one received his scorn like the religious leaders of his day.

Rather, time and again, Jesus told his followers that he came to serve and not be served, and if they wanted to honor God, they should do the same.

Perhaps Jesus's longest speech on the truest test of discipleship comes in Matthew 25, where he tells the story of the sheep and the goats. In the story, Jesus tells us that the ultimate measuring stick for the kingdom is how we treat people in need. Those who do good works for the poor are labeled the "sheep," and those who do not are called "goats." In telling us who to serve, Jesus holds out the hungry, thirsty, naked, sick, imprisoned, and immigrant as primary examples. "Whatever you did for one of these least brothers of mine, you did for me," he says. The message is so simple and stark that it makes one wonder why we Christians often mistake it for someone else's job.

But the story doesn't end there. If it did, it would probably go down as a nice little story about how we're supposed to help the poor when we can fit it into our schedules and pocketbooks. The story has a lot more punch than that.

When the goats of the story protest that they haven't done anything for Christ because they never saw him sick or hungry or thirsty or naked, he says quite plainly that "when you refused to help the least of my brothers and sisters, *you were refusing to help me.*" Ouch.

As Christians, we are called to be Christ's for one another. In Matthew 25, the actions required for that are laid out in simple, plain language. If we do good things for the poorest among us, we do them for Jesus as well. And just as importantly, if we don't help the most vulnerable, then we make ourselves exactly that in the eyes of God.

I'm not sure if the story of the sheep and the goats is supposed to be uplifting or a warning. Maybe it's both. But as members of the richest society the world has ever known, I think it should haunt us more than anything.

Tonight, one billion incarnations of Christ will go to bed hungry, some within a few miles of my house. Something tells me that one day I may have to account for why the granite countertops were so necessary.

26. Letta

There is a man named Letta who works in the yard and garden at Open Arms. I believe he is in his mid-fifties. He was one of our very first employees. More importantly, he is one of my heroes in life.

Letta works hard every day. His main responsibility is working in our large organic garden, which supplies all of our vegetable needs throughout the year. Letta plants the seeds, pulls the weeds, and irrigates the soil. He also feels the joy of harvesting the bounty, giving it to our kitchen staff so everyone can enjoy what he works so hard to provide for us. Letta does an awesome job in the garden, but that is not why he is a hero to me.

I have driven Letta to his home after work, and I have picked him up many times in the morning. He lives down the hill in a township that locals call "the location." The location is like so many other townships throughout South Africa. Some people live in simple concrete homes, others in ramshackle shacks. Letta and his wife live in a shack. It has no plumbing or running water, and it looks like a good wind would bring it to the ground. Yes, Letta lives in a shack, but that is not why he is a hero to me.

Letta is an ordained minister of some sort. In South Africa, there are so many informal Christian churches that it's hard to keep them all straight. Regardless, Letta is close to the Lord, and he often leads prayers at our staff meetings and gatherings. We had a couple once ask for a blessing for their marriage, and Letta did the prayer. Letta speaks fervently and intensely when he prays, but since he prays in Xhosa, I don't know what he's saying. Our staff and children listen closely, so I know they must be good prayers. You can tell a good prayer even if it's spoken in a language you don't understand. Letta lives his life with God by his side, but that is not why he is a hero to me.

Letta is a hero to me because of his attitude. Letta lives in a shack, pulls weeds for a living, and yet always has a smile and a kind word for me or anyone else. He doesn't have a toilet, and yet you do not hear complaints of any kind coming from his lips. If you give him a new shirt or cap or shoes to work in the garden, he will thank you over and over. When we go on a family trip every three years with all the children and staff, Letta is the happiest guy on the bus. He truly enjoys seeing new things and doing things that he never thought he'd do: eat in a restaurant, stay in a hotel, take a cable car to the top of a mountain.

All of us have circumstances beyond our control in our lives. Where we are born, who raises us, health issues, appearance, and many other things are clearly out of our control. But the one thing that we can control every day is our attitude about those circumstances. And that is why Letta is a hero to me.

Letta works in a garden pulling weeds. He gets paid about $300 per month. He lives in a shack with his wife. In his home, he goes to the bathroom in a bucket. He has no retirement plan, very little savings, and he has to walk to work. For him, owning a car is just a pipe dream. He is also one of the most gracious, kind, and positive people that I know.

Heroes come in all shapes and sizes. One of them is exactly the same shape and size as a gardener I know. I look up to him as much as I do anybody.

27. Spiritual Poverty

Several years ago, I watched a PBS television program featuring Dr. Wayne Dyer. Dr. Dyer was a teacher on spiritual matters, and I have avidly watched his programs and read many of his books over the past few decades.

On this particular program, Dr. Dyer told a story about Mother Teresa's visit to Phoenix in February 1989. The story involved an interaction that Mother Teresa had with local radio personality Pat McMahon. Pat is a fixture in the broadcasting business in Phoenix and has done innumerable good things in our community, especially for the less fortunate and the arts. I was curious to talk to Pat about his experience with Mother Teresa to verify Dr. Dyer's story. For many years, I have believed that the story had a very strong connection to the mission of Open Arms Home for Children.

Thankfully, Pat and his wife, Duffy, are long-time friends of my own friend and client Ron Frost. Ron is a wonderful man who has been supportive of our family's work at Open Arms since its inception. When I called Ron to ask if he could connect me with Pat and Duffy to inquire about the story, he was more than happy to oblige. I spoke with the McMahons on the phone about their shared experience with Mother Teresa so many years ago.

In 1989, Mother Teresa visited Phoenix to help dedicate a facility that her order, the Missionaries of Charity, was opening to address the homeless problem in the community. Because Phoenix has warm weather year-round, there is a particularly large homeless problem. Like so many other places in the world with people in dire need, Mother Teresa and her nuns showed up to help.

As local community leaders, Pat and Duffy were invited to meet Mother Teresa at the dedication of the new facility. They both remember two impressions they had upon meeting her: First, that she was very small in stature, standing less than five feet tall. Second, they remember she had an unbelievable presence despite her size. As Duffy told me, "Pat and I both felt her presence the moment we entered the room to meet her."

Upon meeting Mother Teresa, Pat immediately asked how he could help her. As an Irish Catholic and a friend of the needy in our community, that was not an usual question for Pat. The response he got floored him.

"Yes, you can help," Mother Teresa replied. "Go find someone who has no one and love them."

Pat recalls those words today with the same depth of feeling he experienced twenty-five years ago. To Pat, the message sounded exactly like something a saint would say.

In my mind, this wonderful story illustrates two things that made Mother Teresa great. First, Mother Teresa thought human beings were at their very best when they simply reached out to one another in love. Mother did not believe this was best done by large organizations but by individual human beings reaching out to others to overcome their various forms of darkness. She didn't want us to wait for a global nonprofit organization to do work that needed to be done. She felt we all had an individual responsibility to help, and I'm pretty sure that's why she gave Pat the personal instruction to find someone who felt all alone and do the needed work himself.

The second reason I love the story is that Mother Teresa realized that there is a greater poverty than having no place to sleep and no food to eat. She spent her life battling the greatest forms of material poverty, but she said many times that was not the worst kind of poverty. The worst kind of poverty was even more profound and represented a spiritual poverty—namely, that kind of poverty where a person knows neither the love of God or neighbor, suffers greatly, and feels they are all alone in the world. Her instruction to Pat was designed to strike at the heart of that kind of poverty. "Go find someone who has no one and love them," she said. She knew all too well that homeless or destitute people often feel that no one seems to care whether they are dead or alive, and they don't feel the love of God as a result. If Pat helped one of these people in Phoenix, it would of course include support like food and drink, but it would also strike at the crushing loneliness that such people often feel.

Reflecting on this powerful story today, it puts our work in South Africa into simple focus. At Open Arms, our mission is very simply to reach out to orphaned children who have no one and to love them. Every day, we try to carry out the profound instruction that Mother Teresa gave to Pat. It is a privilege to do so.

No child should be without food, shelter, and someone to provide basic needs. But far more importantly, no child should be all alone. They must know they are loved.

28. Yin and Yang

Before we purchased the farm on which Open Arms now sits, I spent a week in Cape Town touring various homes for children to see how orphans were being cared for in different settings. It was a very good experience because it brought into perspective not only the scope of the problem but the many different models of care.

During that week, I stayed in a bed and breakfast in Stellenbosch, a town outside of Cape Town. Stellenbosch is known for its university and for the many wineries in the surrounding area. Little did I know that when I made the reservation, I would be staying at the home of the former mayor of Stellenbosch, a very nice man named Willie Meyer. Willie and his wife Frances were very gracious hosts, and once they learned of our family's plans, they put the wheels in motion to help me meet with community leaders and activists. It was another of those meaningful coincidences: I make a reservation at a B&B, and it happens to be at the former mayor's house!

Willie had a son who was an Anglican priest not too far from Stellenbosch. His son wanted to take me to a home for disabled children that he knew existed outside of one of the townships in the area. Apparently, a heroic local woman had been moved by the plight of disabled children who lived in the townships, and she wanted to give them a better life. Life in a township for a family can be exceedingly difficult when everyone is healthy. Throw in a child with spina bifida, cerebral palsy, or other disabling conditions, and it turns a very difficult life into an overwhelming challenge. One by one, this woman had taken in such children to give them a place to live with running water, electricity, and at least some medical care. She was one of the many extraordinarily heroic people I have had the privilege of meeting in South Africa. Many of the children in her care would have been dead without her efforts.

As we drove to the home, little did we know what lay ahead.

Arriving at the home in the middle of a low-income area, it was apparent that this was not going to be a posh facility. From the outside, the facility looked to be about a thousand square feet in size—the kind of home that might have three small bedrooms and one bathroom. Looking at the facility from the outside, Willie and I thought it must be home to maybe eight or ten children. We looked forward to seeing what this place was all about.

Upon entering the front room, we were greeted by a young female volunteer from Germany. She welcomed us warmly and told us she would be happy to show us around. We went down a small hallway and came upon the first bedroom. In it, there must have been twelve baby cribs, each with one or two children in them. When I saw how they were jammed together, I thought that they must be cleaning the other bedrooms so they temporarily had put all the cribs together in one room. I quickly learned that was not the case.

For the most part, the children were severely disabled. They sat in their cribs and waited for us to go around the very narrow passages in the room to greet them. As you might expect, the smiles we got were big, and the joy at seeing visitors was real. That's when Willie and I started wiping our eyes. We didn't stop until we left the place.

As we toured the other two bedrooms, we learned that all of the bedrooms were jammed with children and cribs and that this tiny house had more than forty disabled children living there. The children were one or two to a crib, and most of them were unable to stand up or walk. They just sat there, each waiting for us to come and greet them. I was so overwhelmed that I could barely talk.

Many experiences in third-world settings take us so completely away from normal life that they both inspire and haunt us forever. This was one of those experiences. To this day, I can't characterize my visit there because it was filled with so many positive and negative emotions at exactly the same time.

The Chinese have the symbol for yin and yang that means "shadow and light" to describe how polar opposites or seemingly contrary forces are connected. For example, the concept of light cannot be understood if darkness didn't exist. The concept of yin and yang was on display in the starkest way possible in that little home with more than forty children crowded together in cribs in three tiny rooms.

There was so much to feel at that home that was not good. There were kids jammed together and living in incredibly cramped conditions that no fire marshal would ever approve. There were about four people working there that day, and caring for so many profoundly disabled children seemed like an overwhelming task. Many of the children were waiting to have their diapers changed, so you can imagine what sensory experience that caused. The children were starved for attention, or so it seemed, and their disabling conditions and the cribs they sat in meant the children could not move to see us. Instead, they waited like animals in cages for us to come by and greet them. Try as I might to erase the thought in my head, I could not help but think of an overcrowded zoo with animals in cages that were far too small. As I thought of this, I continued to wipe my eyes.

On the flip side, it was not hard to imagine most of these children being dead if not for the founder of the home and for the workers. Most of the children were profoundly disabled, and I could not imagine how their families could care for them in shacks with no water, toilet, or electricity. This home was keeping them alive and showing them love of neighbor despite meager resources and overwhelming odds. You could tell the staff loved the kids and did their best to provide for them. I could not help but be inspired by this wonderful and simultaneously horrific place.

We visited the home for no more than twenty minutes. It was about the most emotionally exhausting twenty minutes of my life. I was inspired by the founder and staff, overwhelmed at the conditions, horrified that children lived in cribs that looked like cages, filled with compassion for the "least of" my brothers and sisters, angry that the place didn't have more support from the first world, uplifted by the German volunteer who worked for nothing in such conditions, grateful that such a place existed for the children but profoundly sad at the same time. Now, many years after seeing the place, I must admit that I am still overwhelmed by the experience. It continues to haunt and inspire me at the same time.

In the middle of a poor neighborhood in Cape Town there sits a tiny building that is home to forty or fifty disabled children. They are loved, and they are alive, and they live in cribs that look like cages. May God bless that place in all its horror and humanity and tragedy and hope. Saints live there and so do disabled and disfigured children—both of whom will be way ahead of the rest of us in the line to get into heaven.

Mother Teresa said we are all called to serve God "in all his distressing disguises." I fully understand that challenge she laid before us. I have never seen a place so distressed and so uplifting at the same time.

29. Playing It Safe

Starting Open Arms was very risky for our family. We took all the money we had and gambled that it would produce good fruit. We had more questions than answers, more things to learn than we actually knew. We figured it was a risk worth taking because so many children were suffering, but it was still quite a gamble. We figured God would bless the project, but we got nothing in writing that he would actually do so.

So much about life these days seems to be about safety. We have insurance for our cars, our homes, and our lives. We have health insurance in case we get sick. We have retirement plans to make sure we don't outlive our assets. We have air bags if we get in a car accident and home security systems to protect our homes. We own guns to "keep us safe." We have disability insurance in case we get disabled and flood insurance in places like Arizona, where it hardly ever rains.

We have all these things not because we want to spend money on them. We have them because we live our lives in fear. Fear is sold in advertising because after all, only fools take risks they don't have to take. And like sheep, we line up to buy whatever will make us safer, hoping to protect ourselves in so many ways we can't even count them all. Fear gets the best of us in our minds and in our wallets.

In the Bible, the most commonly found command is not "love each other." It is the simple two-word command "fear not." I once read that there are 365 different "fear not" commands in the Bible—one for each day of the year. I believe they exist in such abundance because God realizes—and we should too—that fear often prevents us from living the lives we are meant to live. We play it safe, fearful of the consequences of stepping out in faith, hope, or love.

In the Gospels, there is the story of a rich young man who meets Jesus and asks what is necessary to inherit eternal life. Jesus tells him to keep the commandments. The young man says he has done that all his life. But then comes the kicker: Jesus tells him to also sell all that he has and give it to the poor. The rich man, the scripture says, "went away sad because he had great wealth." Fear got the best of the young man. He couldn't risk his possessions, even if it meant eternal life.

I often think about that young man. Did he grow old and regret not risking it all for the grand adventure that Jesus offered to him? Did he grow bitter late in life, realizing that his possessions offered him shallow satisfaction? It would be good to know the rest of the story.

The truth is, we all cling to something just like the young ruler did. It may not be our possessions; it may be our public image, our job, our perceived safety. Fear holds us back even when the good book says "fear not" so often that it reeks of overkill.

In a book called *God, But I'm Bored!,* author Eileen Guder wrote:

> You can live your life on bland food so as to avoid an ulcer, drink no tea, coffee or other stimulants in the name of health, go to bed early, stay away from night life, avoid all controversial subjects so as to never give offense, mind your own business, avoid involvement in other people's problems, spend money only on necessities and save all you can. You

can still break your neck in the bath tub, and it will serve you right.

Amen, sister!

The fruit on a fruit tree is always found on the end of the skinny branch. If we want to taste the fruit of the tree, we have to go out on the branch and get it. That always involves risk. But as the rich young man who encountered Jesus reveals, the ultimate risk is not taking one at all.

"Nothing ventured, nothing gained" is an old saying. A truer saying might be "nothing ventured, something lost."

Every day, I thank God for the children at Open Arms. I am grateful that they have a home and for the utter foolishness God gave us to get it going. As the children abundantly prove, it was a risk worth taking.

30. A Letter from Bobo, Spring 2011

Like most people, I have a very special place in my heart for my mother. She died when I was twenty-four years old, but I still cherish every single memory I have of her. She was a joyful, funny, and compassionate person who touched the lives of everyone she encountered. Not a day goes by without me thinking of her in some way.

Regardless of when it happens, the loss of a mother is a very traumatic event. Moms are very special people because they bring us into the world and have a bond that no one else can have. They literally give us the gift of life.

At Open Arms, many of our children experience the trauma of two separations from their mothers. The first one takes place when mothers become too sick from HIV/AIDS to care for their kids and the children are placed with us. The second one, unfortunately all too common, is experienced sometime later when the mother succumbs to AIDS and passes away. In the past year or so, we have had eleven children lose their mothers to the scourge of AIDS. This is more than one-quarter of the children in our care. The children attend the funerals, and we do our best to help them through love, counseling, play therapy, and a lot of hugs. These actions are never enough, but we do our best to let them know that their mothers have moved onto a better place and that they still have a home where people love them.

South Africa has one of the highest rates of HIV/AIDS in the world. More than 20 percent of the adults in a population of 49 million are HIV positive. For that reason, we know that we have not seen the last of the children coming to our doors because their mothers are sick nor the last of the funerals that follow. This is the reality we face.

Your gifts to Open Arms provide love and hope to kids who have experienced the loss of a mother far earlier than most of us. That's why your support is so critical and so appreciated. We cannot and do not replace the special love that only a mother can provide, but we do our best, and I know firsthand how much the children appreciate it and how much difference it makes in their lives.

There is a Jewish proverb that says "God could not be everywhere, so he created mothers." In their absence, our children are very grateful that he created *you.*

31. I Promise to Sing to You ...

I love music and often find great meaning listening to it. I have absolutely zero musical talent myself—the only thing I can play at all is the radio. But my utter lack of musical ability doesn't stop me from enjoying music any more than it stopped my grandmother from following the Cubs every day of her life, even though she couldn't play baseball worth a lick. (For obvious reasons, I think music brings me more joy than the Cubs did for my grandmother. The team has had a particularly bad century!).

I especially love listening to songs with good lyrics. You can take a lot of meaning from lyrics because, like poetry, they often have great depth.

A few years ago, a group named Train came out with a song entitled "Marry Me" that I find simply beautiful. In it, the singer proclaims loyalty to his love and asks her to "marry me today and every day." I love that line because it shows the commitment that people who love each other must have to renew their love each and every day. It's not just about the wedding day but about every single day that God gives us to honor and serve each other.

That's why "new" love is special, but the deepest love is always "old" love tested by years of trials, joys, and everything in between. I am always inspired by couples who have loved and served each other for decades, having decided to do so despite the tragedies, hardships, arguments, and struggles they have undoubtedly lived through.

Despite my Spanish last name, I'm 100 percent Irish. My mom once told me that being Irish means we laugh *and* cry twice as much as people of other nationalities. I think she was right, and nothing seems to make me cry more than people who have devoted their days to each other and stick to that commitment no matter what. To me, "old" love among couples is the surest proof to me that we are created in God's own image. He loves us just the same way and even more. He will never, ever abandon us or turn away from us.

Towards the end of "Marry Me," the singer sings one of the most beautiful lines I have ever heard in a song. He says, "I promise to sing to you when other music dies." I absolutely love that line, and it is so true of the commitment of married life. Every couple faces the death of family members or friends, financial struggles, arguments, and moments when the music of our lives is interrupted or seems lost forever. At such times, husbands and wives turn to each other and sing to each other in ways that no one else can. It's what makes marriage among the great privileges a human being can have.

As people of faith, we are called to do exactly the same thing for others in need—promising to sing to them when other music dies. That calling is not just confined to marriage but to everyone we share this planet with.

When I listen to "Marry Me," of course I always think first of my wonderful wife, Sallie. She often sings to me when other music has died, and I am grateful every day for that. But I also think of the children at Open Arms because our mission is simple: we sing to children every day because other music *has died* in their lives. The song we sing is indeed a love song, not a replacement for the ones their parents would have sung but certainly a love song nonetheless. It is a great privilege to sing this love song for them. And best of all, every single day they sing it right back.

32. Flour and Water

....

We have a boy named Themba who came to us at nine days of age. He was born to a mother who abandoned him on the second day of his life and then left town. Like many of the circumstances that lead children to Open Arms, we're not sure why this happened. Maybe it was drug or alcohol abuse, or maybe it was just a reaction by a far-too-young mother to the responsibility of caring for a child.

The next-door neighbor, an elderly woman, found the child alone in a shack and began caring for him. She didn't know what happened to the mother and knew the child would die without care. I have come across many such stories since we started Open Arms: people start caring for kids in their neighborhood not because they are related or because they want to but merely to keep the child alive. It is quite a burden for impoverished neighbors, but they don't know what else to do.

The elderly woman who took in the child was so poor that she could not afford baby formula and was obviously unable to breastfeed Themba. So she fed him what she had in her house—a mixture of flour and water.

With such a diet for about a week, Themba quickly became deathly ill. The elderly woman took him to the local health clinic and told his story to the nursing staff. It was not the first or last time a story like that was told at the clinic.

Later that day, nine-day-old Themba was referred by a local magistrate to Open Arms Home for Children. He is now five years old and is completely healthy.

In grade school, we used to make paste out of flour and water. Every time I look at Themba, I cannot help but think about the diet of paste that started his life and almost killed him. And then I think of his neighbor who tried to keep him alive with the meager resources she had. She did her very best, and it was her heroic action that led him to a better life.

At Open Arms, so many circumstances have a conflicting, yin-and-yang quality to them. A boy is born—good. He is abandoned after twenty-four hours—tragic. He is cared for by an elderly neighbor who doesn't know what to do—great. He is fed paste because that's all she has—sad. She takes him to the clinic, and he ends up at Open Arms—good.

In the last ten years, I've learned that life at the margins has so many conflicting messages. Nothing seems to go as planned, and tragedy and heroism are so intertwined that you often cannot get your mind around what's happening.

Komga, South Africa, is about ten thousand miles away from my home in the suburbs. But it often seems like it's on a different planet. Stories like Themba's merely confirm it.

33. Father …

At Open Arms, something happens every single day that will make you laugh out loud. Whether it's a child making a joke, saying something unintended, or just being silly, you cannot go a single day without a good laugh of some sort.

Fr. Billy Barnes is a Catholic priest who is a good friend and has been particularly helpful to us in a number of ways. He has a terrific sense of humor and has served God with humility and laughter for more than fifty years.

One day, Father Barnes dropped off some sweaters that local nuns had knitted for the kids. They were beautiful and were sorely needed for our cold South African nights. South African homes like ours have no central heat so it can get chilly, even inside.

Upon coming home from school and not finding a new sweater on his bed like the other kids, one of our boys asked Rita, our executive director, a most straightforward question: "Why didn't I get a sweater from Father Bum?"

Now you must know that in South Africa, "bum" is often the word that is used for rear end! We could not stop laughing, and the only thing better than hearing about the sweaters from "Father

Bum" was telling Fr. Barnes about his new name! He laughed even harder than we did!

At Open Arms, God grants us good humor to get through days filled with the often overwhelming activity that caring for more than fifty children provides. Long live Father Bum!

34. Generosity

A farmer named Nelson Henderson once said that "the meaning of life is to plant trees under whose shade you do not intend to sit." In other words, one of life's greatest riches is to help people without expectation of repayment or personal gain.

One of the most remarkable aspects about Open Arms is the way that our extraordinary donors share of their resources to help children they will never even meet. It is so humbling to witness this, and it is clear that they live out Henderson's definition of the meaning of life.

Since even before Open Arms opened its doors, people have been stepping up to give of their resources so that kids on a small hilltop in South Africa can have a better life. Our donors come from all backgrounds and ages, all faiths and colors. But they share a common belief that children should not be alone and that our work is worth supporting.

The generosity of our larger donors is so inspiring to see. In fact, I am often just as inspired by their giving as I am by the children they help. Sallie and I often get teary-eyed when a large gift is received, often with an encouraging note. "Keep up the great work," they'll write, not realizing that the great work is a direct result of their gift. One of the realities of nonprofit work is that money makes it happen, and the money must come from people who are generous in spirit and deed. Knowing such incredible people is just as rewarding for me as serving the children. It is truly inspirational to know people who are so generous and so alive in their hearts and deeds.

The same inspiration, however, can be drawn from some of our smaller donors. Children have bypassed birthday gifts and instead directed that the money for gifts be given to Open Arms. Vacation Bible Schools raise money through coin collections. It's amazing to see how much money a hundred kids can find in the couches at their homes! Retirees on fixed incomes give regularly when in many ways, they can't afford it. People have sent us twenty dollars or fifty dollars they found on the street and figured their good fortune was God's way to help orphaned children. These kinds of gifts are just as inspiring as the larger gifts, and they also have a huge impact on the lives of our kids.

Generous donors, big and small, are some of the most unbelievable people you will ever meet. They spend their lives planting trees under whose shade they do not intend to sit and I know—absolutely *know*—that they will not go without their reward.

35. An Awesome Responsibility

....

Two of the first children who came to Open Arms were Khanyisa and Kwame, two brothers who were living on their own prior to coming to us. They were living on their own because their mom was too sick with AIDS to care for them. For a couple of months, the boys, aged nine and three, begged to stay alive. It was a very difficult situation that was chronicled in a very moving article in the East London newspaper.

After the article came out, local social workers intervened and placed the boys at Open Arms. Like all of our children, they came to us with only the shirts on their backs, hoping for a better life than the one they had been living. Thankfully, they found it.

Khanyisa and Kwame were two very spirited children. They were leaders among their peers at Open Arms, and they quickly picked up English as their second language. After a few months, they had settled in nicely and were doing well.

After the boys were with us for a while, our Executive Director, Rita Montgomery, took them to the hospital to visit their ailing mother. Rita reported that the boys' mother was emaciated from AIDS and truly looked like she was going to die any day. In some African countries, the slang word for AIDS is "slim," and that described the boys' mother. She could not have weighed more than seventy pounds.

When Rita and the boys visited her in the hospital, she was unable to hug her two sons because she didn't have the strength to raise her arms. Rita said it was very moving to see the two boys kiss their mother goodbye for what she assumed would be the last time. Unfortunately, in our work in South Africa, such scenes are not uncommon.

On a subsequent visit to Open Arms about four months later, I was startled to learn that the boys' mother had made a remarkable recovery thanks to antiretroviral medication. She slowly regained her strength and was released from the hospital. I was amazed one afternoon to see her walking our grounds and visiting with her two sons. In just four months, she went from too weak to give a hug to being able to walk around our campus. It was one of the most remarkable comebacks from illness that I have ever seen.

Once she was stable enough to provide for her sons again, plans were made to reunite the boys with their mom. Children should be with their parents, even if conditions are less than perfect. Kwame and Khanyisa's mom lived in a tin shack with a dirt floor and no plumbing or running water, but it was home, and she wanted to have her sons return as soon as they could. As a parent myself, I certainly understand that.

The boys, however, had come to feel that Open Arms was their home and had very mixed feelings about returning to live with their mom. This was completely understandable, as home reminded them of the trauma of living on their own and begging to stay alive. They loved their mom, but the thought of going back to the same conditions they had lived through was frightening.

Our staff prepared the boys the best they could for the day when they were to go home. I was not present on the day they left but was later told about what happened. Apparently, when the social worker came to take the boys home, they did not want to go. Kwame, the youngest boy who was three years old, was too young to know what was happening, but he took his cue from his older brother, who would not get in the car to return home. Khanyisa, ten, had been so traumatized by living on his own with his younger brother that he wanted no part of returning to the scene of so much suffering. He loved Open Arms because he didn't have to worry about the next meal or not having a place to sleep. On top of that, he had been able to attend school for the first time in his life. He just didn't want to go to a place where that might not continue.

Because I loved those boys so much, it would have been so difficult to see them torn in such a deep way. I was told that after considerable coaxing, the two boys were put in the car, and it slowly started down our driveway. Khanyisa, the older brother, rolled down the window and yelled to the other children, "Please tell Bobo about this! He would never let this happen! Please tell Bobo about us!" The car headed out of earshot, and the boys were on their way back home.

When I was told about this episode from one of the older children in our care, I cried. The children put so much trust in us, and in Khanyisa's mind, I would have saved the day for him and his brother. This, of course, was not true, but I could not help but feel that I should have been there to tell him it was going to be OK.

Since that time, I often visit the boys and their mother at their home. It is clear that it is a tough existence but the boys are back where they should be. I often bring a small gift to help the family out, but more importantly, I bring a hug for the boys to let them know that they are not forgotten and they remain important members of the Open Arms family. They have lost their English skills for the most part, but they are always happy to see me, and I'm even happier to see them.

Hearing about Khanyisa screaming, "Bobo would never let this happen" still moves me. It serves as a very real reminder of the awesome responsibility we have to look out for the children in our care. The children trust us with their lives—literally—and it is a heavy and awesome responsibility.

Every single day, I hope and pray that we live up to the trust that the children place in us. The world does not give children like Kwame and Khanyisa a voice of any kind. We adults have to be their voice, and they trust us to use it well.

Outside of caring for my own wife and children, it is the most important job I will ever have.

36. Loaves and Mattresses

In the Gospels, we read about how Jesus fed hundreds of people by multiplying five loaves and two fish. It is a remarkable story about how God can do anything, including making things multiply, whether it is food or love or joy. Remarkably, I have learned that the story applies equally to mattresses.

In August of 2005, Sallie and I took all the money we had to buy Highstead Farm, a seventy-acre property in Komga, South Africa. It was a beautiful hilltop property complete with a home, two cottages, a tennis court, a swimming pool, and lovely views of the surrounding countryside. The town doctor was selling the property, and it seemed like a perfect place for a home for children. We had $220,000 saved up, and the farm cost $218,000. Some things are just meant to be.

On my first visit to the property after we purchased it, I spent a week sleeping on the only furniture left in the in the home by the previous owner: an old mattress left in the main bedroom. It was pretty comfortable, and thankfully I had a thick blanket to ward off the cold winter evenings on that first stay.

When I went to bed for the first time on the mattress on the floor, I prayed to God that he might multiply mattresses at Open Arms in the same way he had multiplied loaves and fishes in the

Bible. I prayed that prayer because I knew that more mattresses on our campus meant more places for orphaned children to sleep at night. Sallie and I had spent all the money we had, so I knew that any more mattresses would have to come from God and from caring people who wanted to help.

It is now 2015, and there are more than eighty mattresses at Open Arms Home for Children! Most of these are used by children, but some are used by volunteers and staff. Some twenty remain unslept on, waiting for additional children and the funding we need to provide love to seventy children.

I have read about the story of the loaves and fishes many times. I find it awe inspiring. But to me, it has nothing on the miracle of the multiplication of mattresses that I have witnessed firsthand.

God lives!

37. Never

As you might imagine, the children at Open Arms come to us for a variety of reasons. Many are orphaned by the HIV/AIDS crisis that grips South Africa. Others are removed from their homes for reasons of abuse or neglect. Some others have come to us after being abandoned by desperate adults

In early 2012, we received a call asking if we had room for a few more children. Having just completed our new dining hall, which allowed us to expand, we were thankfully in a position to take in a few more kids. The social worker on the phone indicated that twin one-year-old children, a brother and sister, had been found abandoned in a cardboard box near the bottom of a ravine.

"A cardboard box?" asked our executive director Rita Montgomery.

"Yes, a cardboard box," she was told.

Young children the world over are found in arms, laps, strollers, and cribs. But they should never be found in cardboard boxes. Never.

I have no idea what drove an adult to leave two children unattended in a cardboard box. I am sure that whatever the circumstances, extreme desperation led to such an action. I try not to pass judgment on that. Grinding poverty, sickness, and overwhelming obstacles drive people to do things that are hard to imagine. I have not been in such shoes and cannot say what I would do if faced with the same situation.

But I do know this: children should never be found in cardboard boxes.

Today, the twins, Phumeza and Sipho, can be found where they should be: happily in the arms of loving staff members at Open Arms. They will never return to a cardboard box. Never.

38. Callings

My favorite church song of all time is called "Here I Am." It was written by Dan Schutte, a Catholic priest, and it is based on Isaiah Chapter 6, in which God calls Isaiah to become a prophet. In the story, Isaiah feels he is unworthy of God's call and expresses both doubt and hesitation. But despite those feelings, Isaiah also shows a humble willingness to surrender to his calling, and when God says "Whom shall I send? Who will go for us?" Isaiah says, "Here I am, send me!" (Isaiah 6:8)

Throughout the Bible, stories of callings often have similar narratives. God calls Moses to stand up to Pharaoh, and Moses says, "Who am I that I should go to Pharaoh?" (Exodus 3:11). Moses later says to God, "But suppose they do not believe me or listen to me?" and pleads that he is not eloquent enough for the job. (Exodus 4:1). Later in the Old Testament, God calls Jeremiah, and he responds by saying he is a terrible speaker and too young for the job God is giving him. But like Moses, Jeremiah relents and does the work he has been called to do.

Stories like this in the Bible show us that the natural human response to God's call in our life is often "Who me?" or "Really? Tell me you're kidding." Like the people God calls in the Bible, we find ourselves feeling that we're far too ordinary to be personally called by the God who made the heavens and the earth. We feel those messages from God *must* be for someone else. After all, I'm just a man or woman living in the suburbs. I can't possibly be called by name like Moses. There are no stories in the Bible about a guy named Bob.

One of the central beliefs of most religions is that God is unchanging. If we believe that, then if God called people in biblical times, he must still be doing it today. Instead of Moses it might be some guy named Fred who is an accountant. Instead of Esther it might be Juanita, the mother of three. But have no doubt—God still calls people, and believe it or not, he just might be calling for us.

Rabbi David Wolpe, in his book *Why Faith Matters,* writes of a man who was standing before God complaining about all the pain and suffering in the world. The man asked God why he didn't send more help. God simply replied, "I did send help. I sent *you.*"

We are weak. Poor public speakers. Probably too old. Maybe too young. Busy at work. Constantly running to kids' activities. Too tired. And yet through it all, God still says, "Whom shall I send?" The Bible shows us that it's OK to be reluctant. God may even expect that from us. But reluctant or not, the answer we give with our lives is very simple: We can either say "Here I am" or "Clearly, you must be thinking of someone else."

Either way, there is an awful lot riding on the outcome.

39. A Lot to Live Up To

There is a young girl at Open Arms named Nontembeko who is so honest, so precious, and so innocent that she takes your breath away. She is five years old. To any visitor, Nontembeko is always there to give a hug, a friendly smile, and a kind word. She is so sincere and so pure that it is almost overwhelming. Independently of one another, many different adults have remarked to me about her innate kindness and sincerity. Nontembeko is that striking to people, even when they just meet her for a short time.

When I reflect on the awesome responsibility we have to care for children at Open Arms, I often think specifically about Nontembeko. Are we giving her the most uplifting home possible? Are we doing our best to educate her? Are we providing her with the most loving staff and volunteers that we can find? How can we grow the innate gifts that God gave her so that she continues to be a gift to the world?

God loves all of the children at Open Arms equally. But he gave them different gifts, qualities, and abilities. Our job is to love all the children equally but help them grow uniquely and differently. That is not an easy task when you have so many children to care for. But we do our best.

Nontembeko reminds us that this is work is a tremendous responsibility. I hope and pray that we will live up to who she is. As with all of our children, I don't want to let her down in any way.

At five years of age, Nontembeko is a gift to the world. I humbly ask for your prayers that we won't screw that up. It's an awesome responsibility and one that requires your prayers and God's help.

40. Faith in Action

I am not an expert on South African history. However, I have read several books on Nelson Mandela, a truly heroic figure in twentieth century history, if not the history of the world. Mandela spent nearly thirty years in prison for opposing the system of Apartheid that existed in the country from 1948 through 1994. Apartheid literally means "aparthood," and it was a system of segregating the country into racial groups. This meant that the members of the country's overwhelming black population were not full citizens in their own country. White people got better jobs, controlled the economy, and enjoyed their own beaches, schools, and clubs. Black people, Indians, Asians, and those of mixed race were held in check by a system of cruel laws and an often brutal police force.

Thousands of people were killed, tortured, or imprisoned opposing this system. Nelson Mandela, a lawyer who was one of the leaders of the African National Congress (ANC) that fought the system, was one of them. In 1961, he formed an armed wing of the ANC to oppose the government. In 1962 he was arrested and sentenced to life in prison for sabotage and thereafter lived twenty-seven years in a prison cell, most of those years on Robben Island, the Alcatraz of South Africa. He was forced to work in a limestone quarry and got to see one visitor and receive one piece of mail every six months. His long imprisonment became the source of an international campaign to try to free him from prison and rid the country of Apartheid.

Under great pressure, Mandela was released from prison in 1990, and four years later, in the first truly free election in the country's history, he was elected President of the Republic of South Africa. It was a historic election followed closely in every corner of the world. In a stunning turnabout—a former political prisoner was elected president of the country.

Mandela had been imprisoned for almost thirty years, watched many of his friends die at the hands of the government, and witnessed great suffering by non-whites throughout his lifetime. And yet, when he was elected president, there was no revenge, no retribution, no thought of payback in his mind. Mandela invited the previous white leader, F. W. de Klerk, to be his first deputy in a show of inclusion and reconciliation. As made popular in the movie *Invictus,* he urged the country in 1995 to get behind the Springboks national rugby team, which was dominated by white South Africans.

At the world championship rugby match in 1995, Mandela wore a Springboks jersey with number 6 on it, the number of the white captain, Francois Pienaar. The Springboks won the Rugby World Cup on home soil, and the nation, both white and black, celebrated with unabashed joy. Many of my friends in South Africa recall that day with great pride.

While on earth, Jesus constantly preached about the need for forgiveness. It is certainly one of the commands that Christians have the most trouble following. How else could we explain use of the death penalty? We want people to pay for their sins. Forgiveness is considered a nice thought, but certainly it can't be our policy. Forgiveness is fine, but the gas chamber or electric chair feels a lot better.

Nelson Mandela's life argues for a better way. His tireless work for a free and equal South Africa did not include plans for revenge or getting back at those who made two generations of repression a reality in South Africa. All people were welcome in his government and the new "rainbow" nation that he helped bring about. It's not surprising that the South African constitution that he helped craft is one of the most inclusive in the world, giving constitutional rights to people of all colors, races, and creeds. The constitution gives constitutional rights to gay people, and it forbids the use of capital punishment. It reflects Mandela's belief that all people should live in dignity.

My friends in South Africa, both black and white, speak about Mandela in reverent tones and rightfully see him as a man of extraordinary compassion for both the oppressed and the oppressor. Who else would have invited former captors to have a role in a new government? Who else would have not sought charges and executions for those who executed others? Who else would say that all were welcome in a new South Africa, even those who made the old South Africa so infamous?

I have often read Mandela's speeches, and they are quite understandably filled with references to human rights and equality for all. Rarely have I seen any references to Christianity or religious values. But regardless, actions speak far louder than words, and Mandela's actions show that there is hope for forgiveness after all. His life is a shining example of what Christians should be about, even if we often are not.

There is an old saying that goes, "What you do speaks so loudly that I cannot hear what you are saying." By that measurement, Mandela's life speaks as loudly as any I know. People everywhere, especially those bent on revenge, would be well served to study his life. He exemplifies what "turning the other cheek" is all about, and guess what—it can actually work! In his case, the result is a free and inclusive nation where an "eye for an eye" has been replaced with rights for all and mutual respect among peoples. For those of us who live in societies that insist on killing killers and invading countries to get back for previous attacks, it's certainly a history worth studying and a lesson worth learning, probably for the first time.

41. Winning the Lottery

There is a young boy at Open Arms who has been with us for almost five years. His name is Linda, and he was born HIV positive. His mother died early in his life, and his father is in no position to care for him.

Linda came to us at two years of age in terrible health. He was not on antiretroviral medication (ARVs), and he felt lousy all of the time. His baby teeth were rotten, and his stomach distended. To say the least, he was not a picture of health.

Immediately after he came to us, we put Linda on ARV medication. His health improved within a few weeks, and it was clear he was feeling better. We took him to the dentist, where we were told that the best chance he would have at good adult teeth would require the removal of his baby teeth. We then scheduled Linda for a follow-up session at the dentist.

I happened to be in South Africa the day that Linda had sixteen teeth removed by the dentist. This was the most teeth the dentist had ever removed in one patient in one sitting. It must have been very painful for Linda, but he didn't complain a bit.

When we returned to Open Arms after the dentist, we had to quarantine Linda for a few days because of the blood oozing from his mouth. His HIV-positive status warranted such treatment. But rather than feeling this isolation was a negative, Linda welcomed the attention he got in his own room. For children who live in large families like ours, such individual attention can be hard to come by.

One of the most lasting memories I have at Open Arms came when I presented a popsicle to Linda shortly after he returned home from the dentist. As I came into the room with a popsicle, you would have thought that Linda had just won a million bucks. He smiled ear to ear with not one tooth in his mouth and blood oozing out of his gums. With his bright red mouth, he squealed with delight at his good fortune! Talk about making lemonade out of lemons! For two days, he got all the popsicles he wanted and had someone to look after him one-on-one. It was a glorious couple of days for Linda.

Children have a wonderful capacity to not feel sorry for themselves the way that adults often do. They do not rehash terrible experiences with one another and they do not hold pity parties about the way life has been unfair. Rather, they just wait for the time when they can enjoy some attention and look around the corner for the next popsicle that just might come their way.

I was reminded of this reality in a wonderful way by a two-year-old HIV-positive boy who had bloody gums and not a tooth in his head. To Linda, receiving a ten-cent popsicle was a better than a winning lottery ticket.

I have a college degree from a fairly prestigious university. But I never fail to learn from little teachers like Linda who have come into my life to remind me that I often don't know nearly as much as they do.

42. A Letter from Bobo, Fall 2010

One of my favorite sayings is: "I lamented the fact that I had no shoes until I met the man who had no feet." All of us have problems, and some of them are serious. But realistically, most of our problems range from unexpected car repairs to a lack of money for taking a great vacation.

Last week, I visited Open Arms. The thirty-nine children who call us home are doing very well. Despite the heartbreaking tragedies that our children have lived through, they continue to make Open Arms a place of great joy. Their simple prayers before meals and bed reflect their gratitude for their home and their lives. Strange as it may seem, they consider themselves to be very blessed.

On my visit, a national teachers' strike caused the children to be home all day. As an educational activity, we came up with the idea of making fifty bag lunches with the kids and visiting a local dump where people forage for food every day. Some people actually live at the dump. After announcing this plan to the kids, they were overjoyed with the idea and put great effort into making fifty lunches, complete with bologna and cheese sandwiches, an apple, chips, and a juice box.

The next morning, we headed out early, and the kids joyously took lunches to the people living at the dump. In about fifteen minutes, we had distributed all the lunches, and the children felt very grateful for the opportunity to serve others in need.

Part of the mission of Open Arms is to physically feed, clothe, and shelter children. But a far more important part of our mission is to raise loving human beings who will one day serve God and neighbor as adults.

As our trip to the local dump revealed, our kids are learning valuable lessons every day. Their joy to serve others and their compassion for those less fortunate is proof to me that we must be doing something right.

Thank you for opening up our children to the great possibilities in their lives. In the midst of a scene featuring orphaned children serving food to homeless people in a foul-smelling dump, I saw great hope.

43. Bobby

So many people have an impact on life at Open Arms. Our staff and volunteers do the hard job of raising more than fifty children to be productive South African citizens. Our donors repeatedly give of themselves to ensure that that work can be accomplished. Local people give us sweaters, clothes, shoes, milk, eggs, and other items that we need for the kids. It really is a team effort, and it proves the African proverb that "it takes a village to raise a child." Our "village" of people spans two continents and makes the whole project work.

One of the hardest-working helpers at Open Arms is not a person. He's a cat named Bobby. When we first moved into Open Arms, we had a serious rat problem. This is not unusual for a farmhouse with pastureland around it. What was unusual for me, and especially unnerving, was listening to the rats run around on the ceiling at night while I was trying to sleep. The rats were so large they sounded like dogs running around in the rafters! I don't mind rats, but I just don't want them falling on my bed or running around in my room. Come to think of it, I guess that means I do mind rats.

After a few months of listening to the rats run around at night, we took in our first nonhuman resident at Open Arms: Bobby the cat. He is a gray house cat with stripes, and he loves, absolutely loves, to catch mice and rats. The best part about having Bobby in the early days was that he caught a lot of rats, almost always at night. The worst part was that he would proudly show them off in the kitchen or hallway the next morning. In his early days on the job, that was at least three or four times a week. There's nothing like coming upon a rat carcass first thing in the morning when you just want a cup of coffee. Rat guts have an especially unnerving look to them at five a.m. But Bobby was proud of the job he was doing and loved to show off his work.

Thankfully, after a month or so, the carcasses in the kitchen or hallway became a lot more sporadic. Gradually, Bobby's efforts tapered off considerably because there just weren't any rats to catch. Bobby had done the job.

These days, Bobby still patrols at night and looks for any invaders in the seven buildings where people sleep. Because he has effectively intimidated every rat and mouse within twenty kilometers, there is just not much to catch anymore. So, to prove his worth, he now goes out into the yard or pasture to find the occasional passerby, and of course he drags it to the door or veranda to show that he's still on the job.

The work that goes on at Open Arms is really important. A lot of people come together to make it happen. Thankfully, we also have the help of Bobby.

I sleep a lot better at Open Arms than when we first moved in. Now if we can just train Bobby to get the spiders, we'll be all set.

P.S.: Bobby died in 2012 and has been replaced by Nala and Komga, two equally hard-working cats. Not surprisingly, it takes two felines to do Bobby's work.

44. Imagine

Albert Einstein once said, "Imagination is more important than knowledge. For knowledge is limited to all we now know and understand, while imagination embraces the entire world, stimulating progress." One of the greatest scientists to ever live embraced imagination more than knowledge. And as the self-proclaimed worst scientist on earth, I could not agree more.

Ten years ago, Open Arms existed in one place—my family's imagination. It was nothing more than an idea. Today, that idea is home to nearly sixty children and will be home to ten more in the next few years. But it started in our imagination, not in our knowledge about how to run a home for orphaned children on the other side of the earth. I think this is what Einstein was getting at—every advancement, every project, every breakthrough starts first with an idea, not with knowledge of how to get it done. It was reported that the Wright brothers took five sets of parts out to the field each day, sure that their soon-to-be flying machine would crash and need repairs. But they believed in their imaginations that they would invent a way for people to fly. And so it happened.

Several years ago, I listened to a man named Erik Weihenmayer speak at a conference. Erik has climbed the highest peaks on all seven continents. On May 25, 2001, he stood on top of the world on

Mount Everest. What is most remarkable about these achievements is that Erik Weihenmayer lost his sight at age thirteen and is completely blind. He has accomplished without sight that which the sighted have rarely accomplished.

During his talk, Erik said something that I will never forget. He said, "For most people, seeing is believing. I think they have it backwards. For me, believing is seeing." Who could argue with a blind man who has accomplished so much?

Watching people like Erik accomplish great things, I notice that they all start with a belief in their hearts or an idea in their imagination. They don't start with a hundred-page blueprint of how they are going to accomplish their goal. If we had developed that at the onset of Open Arms, we probably would have been intimidated and given up. But we didn't start with that; we started with a vision of children laughing and playing in a beautiful setting. We believed in that completely and eventually we saw it.

Believing *is* indeed seeing. Imagination *is* more important than knowledge.

If we want to accomplish more, maybe we should take Einstein's advice, put down the science and business books, and read more fairy tales. We might get more done.

45. The Universal Language

I just sat in the lounge at Open Arms and listened to four of our teenage children give each other a hard time. The conversation was between one boy and three girls, and they were ribbing each other in a good-natured way. It was fun to see them trying to top each other with one-liners, every response producing howls of laughter back and forth.

The kids spoke in Xhosa, so I didn't understand a thing. But they spoke in such a way that I pretty much understood everything. People giving each other a hard time is so universal that you don't need to understand the language to be a part of it. I played baseball for twenty-five years, and fun, good-natured insults between teammates are as much a part of the game as hitting and throwing the ball. Such back and forth is part of being on a team or a family, and you don't have to know the language when it is going on. Watching the kids carry on today, no feelings were hurt, but barbs went back and forth like the volleys in a tennis match.

It did me good to see this not only because it is a natural part of banter between people who like each other but because it betrayed a kinship that is important. Only people who are secure in themselves can banter in such a way as to not be offended by the barbs that inevitably come back. And only people who care about each other can throw funny insults while not straying anywhere near what might be considered out of bounds. This is a good sign for kids who have suffered much. They respect themselves, and they respect each other.

For four young people to carry on, unrelated by birth but thrown together by circumstance into a large family, it speaks to the fact that they are getting what they need out of our family at Open Arms. Barbs and jabs are thrown and taken by people secure enough in themselves to take the heat and yet respectful enough to not go for things that cut anywhere close to the bone. This is a part of any family on earth, and I didn't have to know Xhosa to appreciate it.

Upon leaving the room after fifteen minutes of being a silent witness, I said my first words and told the boy that he should know better than to start an argument with three girls who have lots of dirt on him. It's only common sense, regardless of the language you speak.

46. The Start

Life is rarely more monumental than when a big dream comes true. And so it came to pass on March 16, 2006. I was sitting at my desk at work in the States when the phone rang. As usual, I answered the phone, "Hi, this is Bob. Can I help you?" On the other end of the phone was Mzwakhe, our director at Open Arms.

"I hope you're sitting down," he said. I was. He told me that ten minutes earlier, we had received our first child at Open Arms. A social worker had dropped off a two-year-old boy who was in need of a home.

For the better part of two years, Sallie and I had planned for this day, but when the call came, it was too much. I sat at my desk and cried.

I often think about that day. The most overwhelming emotion was feeling responsible for another human being. After all, we had not received a puppy! A little guy was depending on us, and to be honest, it felt great to be depended on. God had turned our dream into a reality.

The name of the young boy who came to us means "a lesson" in Xhosa, and I don't think that's a coincidence. Ever since that day, I have learned many lessons from the children who call Open Arms home. They have taught me so much about life, love, resiliency, and joy.

When dreams come true, we feel excited, thankful, humbled, and blessed. That was certainly true on our founding day, March 16, 2006, and it is just as true today.

47. The Tension

I have two jobs. One is to care for my family and clients by working as a financial advisor in suburban Phoenix. I get paid to do that. The other job is to care for my extended family by raising money for the children at Open Arms in South Africa. I don't get paid to do that.

Both jobs are important. Helping people manage their life savings is very critical. I try to not only give my clients financial security but also something more important—peace of mind. I have done the job for twenty-two years, and I am grateful that we have been able to raise and educate five children because of it. On top of that, we were able to get Open Arms going with the fruits of that labor. Finally, I am also glad that Sallie will be in a position to care for herself in retirement. I work with retirees, and I often witness a husband dying long before his wife. I will probably die before Sallie, and I don't want her to face a mountain of worry when that happens. These are important things.

My other job, working as a volunteer for Open Arms, provides no financial security, no retirement, and no insurance. I get paid in hugs.

Many times I have been tempted to exchange my paying job for the non-paying one. I know how many children are suffering.

I have witnessed their plight with my own eyes. So many children in sub-Saharan Africa suffer in silence without parents. There are many statistics on this phenomenon, but I don't need statistics. I have seen it for myself.

This tension, really *the* tension in my life, is often difficult. The work I do for my clients is very important. However, compared to giving a child a home or a future or both, it can lack gravitas. I take my work as a financial advisor very seriously, but it does not involve life or death. For a child who is HIV positive and living without parents, my non-paying job can mean the difference between living and dying. It is hard to keep it all in perspective.

At the end of the Oscar-winning movie *Schindler's List*, 1,100 Jews gather to thank their protector, Oskar Schindler, for saving them from the gas chambers by employing them throughout World War II in factories in Poland and Czechoslovakia. Schindler had given away pretty much everything he had to bribe the Nazis to not murder his workers. In one of the final scenes of the movie, the workers present a letter of thanks and a gold ring to Mr. Schindler to thank him for his extraordinary efforts. He immediately breaks down and asks himself why he didn't sell his car or his gold pin—it could have meant more lives saved. "I could have got more out," he says with eyes full of tears.

Open Arms is a small home on a hilltop in South Africa. It cannot be compared to the efforts of one man to save 1,100 people from certain death. But to be quite honest, there are days that I feel the deep regret of Oskar Schindler. I can only hope that God will forgive me for not doing more. I too "could have got more out."

48. Woe Is Me—Not!

If you hang around adults pretty much anywhere, you will often hear a list of complaints. Someone will tell a story about losing baggage on a plane trip, and then another person will try to top that by saying, "If you think that's bad, let me tell you about the time everything in my luggage was stolen, or eaten by a sea serpent, or how it fell out of the cargo bay at 35,000 feet over eastern Oklahoma." It is a natural human tendency for adults to do this. We exchange stories about difficulties, whether it's how poor we were as kids, how bad our lumbago is flaring up, or how our next-door neighbor died of a heart attack even though he ran six miles a day and had never eaten gravy.

This tendency to share such stories reminds me of the Gary Larson *Far Side* cartoon in which two pirates are talking to each other in a bar and one has obviously finished telling the other guy about why he has a wooden leg. Immediately, the other pirate responds "Well, that's a pretty good story, but let me tell you about the time I got *this*." When you look at the cartoon, the man doing the talking has a peg *head* with a sailor's cap perched above. It's a classic *Far Side* and not too far from the truth of what often happens when we adults talk to each other.

The interesting thing about this phenomenon is that it does not exist among children in any culture that I've witnessed. For example, the kids at Open Arms often have lost their parents, lived through extreme poverty, and known tragedy at a very young age. But you will never, ever hear them talk about how tough it was or say, "If you think that was bad, let me tell you about what happened to me." Children do not think nor act like that.

Wayne Dyer was a very famous spiritual writer and speaker who died in 2015. He wrote several books that I have read. As a child, Wayne bounced from foster home to foster home because of issues in his birth family. In his talks, he remarked that people often said, "Oh, living in a foster home, that must have been terrible." Dyer went on to say, "No, that wasn't terrible at all. When you're six years old, you don't wake up every day and say, 'Oh my God, I'm living in a foster home! How come me and no one else?' You don't do that—you don't do that until you're forty."

There is a great lesson in seeing and reflecting on this remarkable difference between children and adults. Children, even those who have suffered greatly, do not think or talk about how bad things have been. Instead, they get up each day wanting to turn the page to see what might happen next. They do not compare bad stories, and they do not place negative judgments on what has happened to them. They just live in the present.

Children teach us many, many lessons. One of the most important is their complete and utter focus on the moment and their innate ability to turn the page despite difficulty.

It's too bad we adults are often too busy complaining to take full notice.

49. Lessons Learned on the Road

In 2008, I walked across South Africa to raise funds for more cottages at Open Arms. At the time, we were out of space to accept more children. While on the walk, I wrote a daily blog to keep our donors and friends informed of our progress. This was the entry from Day 26, a day spent heading west across the Western Cape Province of South Africa.

Something strange happened on the way to Cape Town today. We started walking, and then walked some more, and then walked some more. Must have been the pasta we ate for dinner last night. Anyway, at day's end, we had walked fifty kilometers—thirty-one miles right on the dot—and most of it into a strong wind. My big question: Is it too late to qualify for the Beijing Olympics? Anyway, with fifty kilometers walked across farm country that doesn't change much, I've decided to change up the blog a bit with twelve lessons I've learned from the South African road. Most of these are life lessons too, but I'll let you draw your own conclusions. So, here goes:

Lesson One: If you're going to go on a journey, it's best enjoyed with a companion. Linda, my walking partner, has become a good friend on this trip. He's committed to completing the journey, and he has a passion for what we're trying to do for our kids in his native country. In my own journey, I'm the luckiest guy in the world to have a wife like Sallie. She is way out of my league, but proof positive that the journey is much better when shared!

Lesson Two: It's OK to stop and rest once in a while! In fact, it is required if you want to complete the journey in one piece. We made it thirty-one miles today, but we wouldn't have come close without a couple of restful breaks along the way. For fast-paced Americans like yours truly, this is a good lesson to learn!

Lesson Three: When you're on a journey, it is hard not see others in need nor to develop a profound sense of gratitude for your own blessings. I passed a lady this morning collecting firewood to keep her ramshackle home warm with a young child on her back. I have never had to do that. A corollary lesson: If you can't see others hurting, then you're traveling too fast and need to slow down and take notice.

Lesson Four: The more you slow down, the more you notice the beauty around you. If I had been in a plane, train, or car, or riding a bike today, I wouldn't have noticed the small purple flowers I saw growing in a rocky area on the side of the road. I wouldn't have seen them at all. It's easier to smell the roses when you slow down enough to appreciate them.

Lesson Five: It's not just the attainment of the goal that makes the journey worthwhile; it's often the view and the experiences along the way. It seems when I just focus on the view and the people I meet on this journey, I am never disappointed. It's all about not missing the forest for the trees!

Lesson Six: In order to get anywhere on a journey, you've got to put one foot in front of the other and get going! There is no journey possible without the first step, no getting to the goal without actually walking. We estimate that we take 50,000 steps each day, but the most important one is always the first one. Mother Teresa wouldn't have picked thousands of people out of the gutter unless she picked the first one up. The smallest activity for a worthy goal is better than the grandest intention.

Lesson Seven: There are going to be obstacles—and sometimes big ones—on any journey. Today, walking in our thirtieth mile, we went up a hill that seemed like Mount Everest. No matter how many hills you go up, there are going to be more hills to conquer. No matter how hard the wind blows in your face, it will blow that hard again one day. You can spend your time cursing the conditions, or you can do your best to overcome them. You overcome them by tackling them head-on and not avoiding the problems. That is how a successful journey takes place.

Lesson Eight: When you're on a journey where others are depending on you, you have more strength to rise to the occasion. My ankles swelled up mightily in the first week of this walk. But with the hopes, prayers, and good wishes of everyone riding with me, I was able to continue. The fact that future residents of Open Arms were depending on me to continue made it even easier to keep going. The best journeys are ones where we carry the hopes and expectations of others with us.

Lesson Nine: If you just keep on going, the journey will provide you with pleasant and unexpected surprises. Today, a rogue ostrich who had escaped an enclosure followed me along the side of the road for almost two miles. Only a fence stopped "Fido" from following further. For that thirty minutes, I didn't think about my legs or the distance remaining or being hungry. Pleasant surprises on a journey will make it more memorable—but only if you keep on going.

Lesson Ten: On a long journey, you have to celebrate the small achievements and milestones you reach. Today, we got within 200 kilometers of Cape Town on our twenty-fourth day of walking. A journey is so much better when you don't wait until the end to celebrate success!

Lesson Eleven: If you're going to have fun on a journey, you have to make your own fun! While a journey will often present some fun along the way, far more often you have to create fun by yourself. If you don't, the journey will seem much longer, and it will not be memorable. Linda's ankles were killing him at the end of today's long walk, so we made the best of it—I carried him over the finish line. With no fun, the journey often turns to drudgery.

Lesson Twelve: The best journeys happen when you are committed to something larger than yourself. Today, we walked a record (for us) fifty kilometers, and I constantly thought about one of our children. She will go unnamed, but she came to Open Arms at about nine months old. Every time we changed her diaper, she screamed bloody murder. After a doctor's visit, we discovered that she had been violated in two ways at an early age. How do you deal with such an outrage? I'll tell you how: you do everything in your power to make sure that child is given all the gentle love she can. You walk up hills like they were nothing, and you do what you can to reclaim that child for humanity and for the God who created her. This is the best lesson of the journey and one that I'm privileged to learn again and again at Open Arms. This blog is filled with lighthearted and hopefully interesting photos of an adventurous journey, but the work we do for children is vitally important. Thank you for being such a critical part of it. I am privileged to have you along on this journey!

See you tomorrow! Bob

50. Luck?

Because I work in the world of financial services, it is not unusual for me to talk to people who are motivated by money—both having it and making it for others. This is certainly not surprising, and I have learned to live with the uneasy balance of working in finance without being controlled by it. I too work for a living and do my best to make money for my clients. But I always try to remember that my career has to take a back seat to my family and my faith.

Several years ago, I was waiting for a flight home from a business conference that I attended in Washington, DC. Sitting in the airport, I took up a conversation with a man who had also attended the conference. He was a major figure in a financial services company, and he asked me about how Open Arms was coming along. I proceeded to tell him it was going well, that we were growing and the children in our care were a privilege to serve.

I then told him about a few things that had recently happened that seemed to be more than coincidental. I told him about a chance meeting with a woman at a public library who ended up giving us $35,000 to build a cottage. He replied, "That's pretty lucky." I then told him about a woman I met randomly on a plane out of Cape Town, South Africa, that had graduated from the same high school as my wife and kids. She just happened to be working for the

US State Department on AIDS relief in South Africa. Again, my acquaintance remarked about our "good luck."

It is truly one of the most remarkable things in life that two people can react completely differently to the same story or set of facts. My acquaintance in the airport saw these chance happenings simply as good luck. From his perspective, these positive developments were just a matter of chance and could have just as easily not happened if not for lady luck.

From my perspective, of course, the things that had happened were not circumstantial but *providential*, proof to me of God blessing Open Arms in some remarkable ways. Too many positive, seemingly chance occurrences happened early in the history of Open Arms for me to think we were just lucky. I took all of these seeming coincidences to be an expression of God's participation in the project. After all, why would God not help *his* children? Time and again in the New Testament, Jesus showed his love for children and often singled them out as being closer to God than adults. To me, it didn't seem farfetched that God would help us in some very practical ways.

As we boarded the plane to begin the journey home, the guy I had been talking to was seated directly behind my seat. He sat down next to an empty seat, and so did I. Just before the door to the plane was closed, the last two passengers boarded. One of the passengers sat next to me, the other next to the businessman behind me.

As the late-arriving passengers sat down next to us, the man behind me tapped me on the shoulder and said, "I can't believe it." I just shrugged my shoulders. To one man, "luck" had struck again. To another, it was another sign of God's providence.

The two men who entered the plane at the last minute were from Africa. It was pretty obvious because they were dressed in traditional African clothing. The man who sat down right next to me was none other than the Nigerian ambassador to the United States. The man who sat next to my acquaintance was his attaché. On the plane, I had a wonderful conversation with the ambassador about Open Arms, about AIDS in Africa, and conditions in Nigeria, the most populous country in Africa.

At the end of the flight, he gave me his business card and said he would be happy to help with our project. He invited me to stop by for a personal visit if I ever made it back to Washington, DC.

As I sat there talking to the ambassador, it was hard to keep my emotions in check. Almost on cue, God had sent one more reminder of his presence, right after I had told someone about similar things happening. My friend attributed it to dumb luck. I knew better.

Luck is for Las Vegas. God is for every place, even on an airplane headed home with an African ambassador sitting right next to you.

51. A Day at a Time

In 2008, I walked 710 miles across South Africa to raise money and awareness for Open Arms. The walk took thirty days, and we were very blessed to raise $250,000 to build four new cottages at Open Arms with the proceeds.

For a person who is used to a very fast-paced lifestyle, spending eight to ten hours walking across a country can be quite an adjustment. Many times, I remember seeing something in the distance and thinking, *In just three short hours, I'll get there!* For those of us who are used to traveling in planes, trains, and automobiles, slowing movement to four miles per hour can make you appreciate the life of a snail, even if you don't feel like appreciating it.

I can distinctly remember the first few days of the walk. We walked twenty-four miles each day, and my ankles quickly started to swell. On my practice walks back home, I had walked eight miles each day in preparation. Little did I know that eight miles a day is hardly adequate preparation for twenty-four! But given my busy schedule, I just couldn't take the time to do more than eight miles. As they say, there is a price for everything, and my ankles paid the price for my lack of preparation. For the first ten days of the walk, every two hours I would stop to elevate my feet and ice my ankles.

It slowed us down, but it was necessary to control the pain and keep moving forward.

To be honest, the physical pain of strolling twenty-four miles a day on swollen ankles was not as big of a challenge as the mental strain of walking for six or seven hours a day and then realizing that we still had 600 or 700 miles to go! At the beginning of the walk, this psychological test was even more daunting than my sore ankles. I would walk all day and then do a mental tally of how many more miles I had to go. Frankly, this was depressing. It also taught me a very valuable lesson.

After about two or three days on the road, I learned that if I kept up the mental math, I was going to go nuts. Here I was on one of the great adventures of my life, and I kept focusing on how many miles were left to go. South Africa is a spectacularly beautiful country, and I was counting miles rather than enjoying them. Seven hours of walking those first few days only left me thinking about the hundreds of hours we had left. So I made a change about three days into the walk—I stopped counting. I started looking around more, seeing the beauty of the country. I decided that on this walk to the west coast of South Africa, I would just keep walking, and one day the Atlantic Ocean would be at my feet. That would be it. The adventure would be over, and I would have both my wits and memories of a marvelous journey in which I was fully present. And guess what—it worked!

I think this lesson from the South African road applies to life. We are raised in such a goal-oriented society, and we are trained to focus on our destinations and not the journey on the way. This focus on results often leads to anxiety. We constantly ask ourselves, "How many miles do I have left to reach my destination?" Meanwhile, the beauty of life passes by as we count our steps to a goal that may never be realized. And even if it does, what is the point if we were not fully present to the joys and beauties of the trip?

I did walk 715 miles in thirty days. It was a pretty good effort for an old fart like me. But more importantly, I actually learned to enjoy the experience but only after I stopped focusing merely on the destination.

On Day 30, I walked almost thirty-two miles through a terrible and cold rainstorm. The wind blew in my face the entire day, and it was bitterly cold. But as I turned a final corner, there I found myself staring at the shore of the Atlantic Ocean. There were tears in my eyes not only because I had reached my destination but also because I had decided to not focus on it twenty-eight days earlier.

Whether on a long walk or in life, great destinations are best attained only when we're fully present on the journey to reach them.

52. The Start of the Day

Throughout the year, Open Arms has a nine-hour time difference with Arizona. Neither place observes daylight savings time. Because of that vast time difference, when I visit South Africa I am usually up at two or three a.m. for the first week. The problem is I only go for a week at a time, so it means I usually get up really early throughout my visits.

There is a very good thing about getting up in the middle of the night on a hilltop in Komga, South Africa. It means I rarely miss a sunrise. This is a good thing because the sunrises at Open Arms are simply spectacular. Two factors make them incredible to watch.

First, Open Arms sits on the highest hill for miles around. To our south and east is a ridgeline of hills in the distance. These hills guard the beautiful valley below us. When the sun comes up, it actually seems to come up far below us. This makes the first light and the colors that follow it so unobstructed that each moment becomes a spectacular painting, every one of them different from the day before.

Second, Open Arms is about twenty miles from the Indian Ocean. Because of this, there are often thin, wispy clouds to our south and east where the sun comes up, depending on the season. These thin clouds serve as reflective mirrors for the sun and create a panorama of colors that never shows up as well in photos as it does to the naked eye. The shades of pink, orange, red, yellow, and blue are simply breathtaking. It's just one of those things you have to see to appreciate. Living in Arizona, I always think that photos of the Grand Canyon don't do it justice. You have to stand on the edge of the canyon to see what it's really like. The same is true for a sunrise at Open Arms.

My grown children often recall that when we saw a great Arizona sunset when they were young children (we were never up for the sunrise), I would tell them that "nobody paints a picture like God." I told them that so they would learn to appreciate the wonder of creation and enjoy the moment. Taking a picture of what we were seeing was not nearly as good as seeing the real thing.

The same thing is true of sunrises at Open Arms. I must have two hundred photos of the sun rising there. They are excellent photos. But the photos cannot hold a candle to sitting out on the porch of our little cottage with a hot cup of coffee waiting for the light show to begin. It makes getting up at three a.m. well worth it.

Because of the work that we do at Open Arms, I often think of it as a holy place. It is holy to me because it's a place where people come with love in their hearts to do good work. The sunrises God gives us each morning only serve to confirm the beauty of the place and of the work being done.

53. The Children of God

As people of faith, Christians are called to recognize that God is in every single human being. For the most part, this is not difficult on an intellectual level. As brothers and sisters of the same Creator, we are called to honor the light of God in each other, whether the other be Christian or Muslim, young or old, immigrant, stranger, or friend. Africans often call this *ubuntu*, or the reality that we all share a deep, common humanity that binds us regardless of our differences. As Christians, we are called to honor that shared humanity and to honor God's presence within everyone on earth.

In daily practice, however, Christ's call to recognize the light in others proves much more difficult. We execute murderers, bomb our enemies, and send drones to do our dirty work against people we don't like, sure that God is definitely *not* in them. We live as if the Bible is a nice little book for the good-hearted and naïve, but hardly a recipe for living. After all, we've learned to be excellent judges about whether someone has the divine within them—and not surprisingly, we usually find God in people who are just like us.

But in reading the New Testament, of course, we learn we shouldn't act so fast. Often in the parables and stories of Jesus, the hero of the story is a person that we normally would not trust or like. The hero of the story of the Good Samaritan is a foreigner that most Jews would have despised at the time. It would be like Juan, the illegal immigrant who just took your son's job, being the hero of a story. We're supposed to believe that he's a hero? Later, we read that Jesus calls a man down from a tree and invites him to deep fellowship—and the guy in the tree is a damn tax collector! Time and again, Jesus shows us that human beings who carry God's presence are often the people we most easily scorn. Stories about the Good Samaritan and the tax collector make us scratch our heads and begrudgingly admit that the divine presence we are supposed to honor is often found in people we dislike.

Reflecting on my life, I have come to the additional realization that the person that we most often fail to recognize as an essential part of God's creation is not the foreigner or the tax collector—it is ourselves. We read that God loves us, that he cares for us, that we have unlimited potential if we only believe in him—and yet we focus on our sins, our faults, our shortcomings, and all the things we can't do. And when we fail to recognize that God is within us, it becomes almost impossible to see that in others too. Such is the state of humanity since Adam and Eve honored the darkness instead of the light. We see the world not as it is but as we are. If we don't recognize our own light, it is hard to see it in others.

One common example of this reality occurs when we think someone is getting too heady or full of themselves. In such situations, we say, "Who does he or she think they are, God's gift to the world?" not realizing that of course, the answer to that question is always an unqualified yes. We all carry God within us. We are all God's gift to the gift to the world, not in a proud way but rather one that recognizes that we are all part of God's plan for his creation.

After walking across South Africa in 2008, I wrote a short book about the lessons I learned from the walk and from the children at Open Arms. I have learned so many lessons from the kids—don't feel sorry for yourself, enjoy every minute, don't worry about tomorrow, hug everyone you can—and the lessons keep coming from the little teachers who show me what's important in life if I'll only pay attention.

It's been almost ten years since we took in our first child, a boy whose name in the Xhosa language means "a lesson." I don't think his name is a coincidence; I've been learning lessons from him and the other children ever since he showed up on our doorstep in 2006.

Perhaps the biggest lesson I've learned from the children is the way they naturally honor the light in everyone. Children are absolutely wonderful in stripping away all the externals that adults spend their lives cultivating. We care about looks, the size of our nose, butt, or bank account, where people come from, what faith they are, the color of their skin, and where they fit in the social structure. The children at Open Arms don't give a rat's rear end about any of those things. They just meet you in the here and now, enjoy your company, and accept you, warts and all. You can come from Timbuktu or Wisconsin, you can be black or white or yellow, you can be rich or poor, a CEO or a street sweeper and they love you just the same. External labels just don't matter. They don't care if you're a Samaritan or even, God forbid, a tax collector.

I think this is why Jesus said we must become like "little children" to enter the kingdom of God. Children tend to give you immediate and automatic credit for having a light within, and it's only later in life, when we become adults, that we start to look for the darkness in each other instead. Children at Open Arms—indeed, children everywhere—just look for your light and share theirs with you. All of the other stuff is just meaningless fluff, exposed for what it really is: superficial Crap with a capital C.

"Jesus called a child over, placed it in their midst, and said, 'Amen, I say to you, unless you turn and become like children, you will not enter the kingdom of heaven.'" (Matthew 18:3)

Every day, I pray that I will honor the light and the essence of every person I meet as much as the children I am privileged to know on our beautiful hilltop in South Africa. Having spent a lot of time at Open Arms, I have come to appreciate that the brightest light on that hill comes not from the sun or moon but from the hearts and souls of its residents. They are the most real and true children of God that I know.

54. Religion

Organized religion is a strange thing. I studied it for seventeen years of Catholic school education, have a degree in theology, and have made it a priority to study it on my own ever since. I have attended Catholic mass almost every week of my life, and I often attend church at six-thirty a.m. on weekdays before I head to work. I draw great comfort from organized religion, and I'm quite sure I'll be a part of it until I draw my last breath.

But the more I study it and the more I live my life within it, the more I am at a loss to explain many of its inherent negative consequences. Organized religion, whether it is mine or someone else's, has led human beings to kill each other, discriminate against people for one reason or another, turn a blind eye to injustice, and led to the abuse of children, the suppression of women. It has often served as the chief reason behind wars, terrorism, and a great deal of human suffering. It seems every group has a handle on what God wants them to do, and often it leads to exclusion, judgment, and suffering for the poor bastards who just don't agree.

During the Civil War, President Abraham Lincoln was asked if he felt that God was on the side of the North in the war. He responded, "Sir, my concern is not whether God is on our side; my greatest concern is to be on God's side, for God is always right."

Reflecting on that quote, I am always a bit skeptical of someone who thinks they speak for God. In just the last ten years, people who claim to be close to God have flown airplanes into buildings, sexually abused children, cheated on their wives, and entered into homosexual relationships when they preach publicly against homosexuality. This is just the start of the list of the actions of those who claim a closeness to God (there is frankly not enough paper available to complete the list).

I have every expectation that this will not change in my lifetime. For example, there are an estimated 38,000 different Christian denominations, each formed because they felt they had an inside track on what it truly means to be Christian. You wonder what Jesus himself would think of this. But regardless, inside and outside of Christianity, people of all colors and faiths will continue to claim that they have the inside track on what God wants and how what he wants should be enforced, even at great cost.

One night several years ago, I watched a TV interview with the Dalai Lama. When pressed by the interviewer to define his religion in one sentence, the Dalai Lama said four words: "My religion is kindness." Frankly, it was the best definition of religion I have ever heard. How revolutionary it would be if all religions adopted such a simple definition and actually lived it out. You can't blow up people if you're trying to be kind to them. You can't abuse children if you're trying to be kind to them. You can't tell women they have no rights if you are trying to be kind to them. You can't tell a gay man that he is going to hell if you are trying to be kind to him. You can't ignore one billion hungry people, or one homeless woman begging on the streets, if you are trying to be kind to them.

Every major religion endorses the concept that God creates human beings. You wonder why so many people in organized religion think that means only "us," no matter who "us" is. Personally, I think we should listen a bit more to the Dalai Lama. His words and actions seem very Christian, even though he is decidedly not.

55. In Our Darkness

Life can be confusing at best and catastrophic at worst. Friends get cancer. Children are hit by cars. Old people die of loneliness. Most of the time, we don't go seeking these things; they find us. Sometimes they come at us head-on like freight trains hurtling through a tunnel. More often, they sneak up like a thief in the night, turning a random Tuesday into a life-altering event.

Meaning at such times can be hard to find. After all, who can explain why a child dies of leukemia? Who can understand why someone goes to the grocery store and gets shot in the head instead? Who can properly comprehend why Dad didn't wake up this morning and never will again?

Such moments strain our souls and send us searching for meaning in the darkness. The love of your life is taken away and you think, *What can I love about life again?*

And then the doorbell rings. The next-door neighbor of the last twenty years, the guy who never offers to shovel the snow in your driveway even though he knows you have a bad back, shows up with a hug and a meat and cheese tray. He doesn't know what to say, and neither do you. But strangely, you accept his act of humanity, even though you feel you will never be fully human again.

And then your pastor shows up, eager to just be there with you, even though you truthfully find him long-winded on Sunday mornings. He offers you condolences, prayer, and most of all presence, because even the pastor is at a loss about what to say to you. He says something about eternal life, but you forget that as soon as the words are uttered. But you never, ever forget that the pastor showed up.

And then your friends come via the knock of the door, the ring of the phone, or the email inbox. Some of what they say is helpful. Some is not. But they come to you in your hour of need and collectively express that what you feel so deeply is not entirely true—you really are not alone to face the pain.

I do not pretend to understand the meaning of life nor what makes it worth living in spite of the pain and loneliness that often crushes us. But I do know this: we get through life together, or we don't get through it at all. Simple acts of *being with each other* often provide the only way out. A hug, a smile, a meat tray, or just a simple kind gesture often pull us through when all seems lost.

I don't know why God permits suffering to enter our lives even when we believe in him utterly and completely. But I do know that he gives us *the gift of each other* at such times to provide a small ray of light amidst the darkness. These connections sustain us when nothing else does, even during those times when we'd rather not be sustained at all.

When we find ourselves in the darkest of places, there often come tiny rays of light in the form of people who love us and care for us. Thankfully, these slivers of light come to us at exactly those times when the Great Light seems most distant.

The greatest gift that life offers on earth is the gift of relationship. We learn this in many ways, but especially when the most meaningful lights in our lives go out.

56. Too Much

Open Arms Home for Children sits high on a beautiful hilltop overlooking the valley below. It also sits on the edge of something else: a tide of poverty and suffering that is simply not found in places like the United States.

As a result, I have had many experiences in South Africa that are not related to any other experiences I have had in my life. Maybe that's one of the reasons that I often feel more alive in Africa; it presents situations that stretch and challenge my beliefs about so many things: life, death, work, purpose, attitudes, and people. To be challenged is to grow, and all of us grow more in new and unfamiliar situations than old, familiar ones.

Several years ago, we had a situation at Open Arms that challenged me, and I wasn't even present to witness it. But just hearing about it was simply too much. Our executive director at the time, Rita Montgomery, told me about it.

One day, we received a call from a local social worker asking if we could take in three more children. This is not unusual. We get calls all the time asking if there is room for more children at Open Arms. We were expanding at the time, so we told the social worker that we could accept the three children. We didn't know much about their situation, only that they needed a home and their ages were nine, nine, and four. The nine-year-olds were twins. The social worker agreed to drop the children off later that week.

When the three children arrived, they came with the social worker and two other people: their mother and their grandmother. Their mother was suffering from AIDS and was obviously very sick. She had been unable to care for her children for months and finally decided it was time to do something about it. She could no longer watch her children suffer and did not want them to see her suffer a painful death that she was sure would come soon. The grandmother was infirm herself and unable to care for the children.

Because of the infirmity of the adults in the household, the children had served as the providers in the family for months. They fed their sick mother, foraged for food the family could eat, and did their very best to provide for the two adults in the household. This is not unusual for the children who come to us; they are often forced into adult responsibilities about twenty years before they could possibly be ready for them. These are called "child-headed households" by sociologists. A better term might be "households where life sucks."

Upon arriving at the home, the three children were immediately overjoyed at the surroundings they saw. They saw lots of manicured green grass, bicycles, a trampoline, warm beds, and plenty of food. Rita reported that they immediately went exploring around the place, happy to have a place like this to live. It sure beat what they had experienced before living in a shack under the pressure to provide for two adults.

The mother, seeing their happiness, cried tears of joy that her children were going to be in a good place. But without question, those tears also had to be filled with overwhelming sadness. This was most likely going to be the last time she would ever see her children. I cannot imagine what she must have been feeling, knowing full well that death would soon come and her children would be raised by someone else. Tears come to my eyes right now as I write about this several years later.

The grandmother, for her part, was in a different frame of mind and was so impressed with the home that she asked if she and her daughter could stay with us too. She saw that life was easier at Open Arms than in a shack in a township and asked what it would take to stay.

Rita, witnessing all of this take place in the span of twenty minutes, could not help but wipe her tears. It was simply too much. The children were overjoyed, not realizing that they wouldn't see their mother again. The mother was happy also to have her children living in a loving home but was undoubtedly overwhelmed due to the knowledge that she would probably never see her children again. The disabled grandmother just knew one thing: this place was better than hers and she wanted to stay.

These kinds of situations are so confusing, so real, so poignant, and so in-your-face that they cannot help but overwhelm you even when you hear about them secondhand. How do such things happen? How can so many profound things be going on at the same time? What is the ultimate meaning of such situations, and what can we learn from them? To state that there are more questions than answers is only too obvious.

Several weeks later, the mother died of AIDS. The drop-off day was indeed the last time the mother ever saw her children. The children attended the funeral and will be at Open Arms until they are adults. They are happy and well-adjusted, and we are proud of their progress. We don't have a lot of questions about their future, but we still have a lot of questions about the day they came.

Life brings us all a lot of unexpected twists and turns. No one is immune from pain and tragedy. But in places like Africa, the distance between joy and devastating tragedy is often measured by the few feet between a disabled grandmother, a deathly-ill mother, and three happy children.

Some things are simply too much to handle.

57. Good Tired

All of us have heroes in our lives. Some of them are parents or teachers or others who have had a big influence on our lives at close range. Other heroes are people we read about or learn about at a distance. Like most people, I have both kinds of heroes in my life.

One of my heroes I learned about from afar is Harry Chapin. Harry was a famous musical artist in the 1970s and early '80s, and he wrote and sang the hit songs "Cats in the Cradle" and "Taxi," among others. These timeless songs are still played on the radio.

Harry was like most other well-known musical artists—he was rich and famous. But unlike almost any other artist I have followed, he did more than half of his concerts as benefits to raise money for a good cause that he believed in. Half of his concerts! Harry's cause was the elimination of world hunger, and he spent his life raising millions of dollars to help feed hungry human beings in the United States and around the world. He couldn't understand why in a world that could feed itself six times over, there were still hungry and starving people everywhere. Unfortunately, a tragic car accident ended Harry's life far too soon at age thirty-eight. But Harry's music lives on and so does his work to end hunger, which inspired thousands of people. In 1987, he was posthumously awarded the Congressional Gold Medal for his inspiring work to end hunger.

On a couple of Harry's albums, you can find a cut named "My Grandfather." It's not a song but instead features Harry talking about his grandfather and about living your life not for a paycheck but for a purpose. Harry talks about his grandfather, but he might as well have been talking about himself. The cut goes like this:

> My grandfather was a painter. He died at age eighty-eight. He illustrated Robert Frost's first two books of poetry, and he was looking at me and he said: "Harry, there's two kinds of tired. There's 'good tired' and there's 'bad tired.'" He said, "Ironically enough, bad tired can be a day that you 'won' but you won other peoples battles, you lived other people's days, other people's agendas, other people's dreams, and when it was all over, there was very little 'you' in there, and when you hit the hay at night, somehow you toss and turn, you don't settle easy."
>
> He said, "Good tired, ironically enough, can be a day that you 'lost.' But you don't even have to tell yourself because you knew you fought your battles, you chased your dreams, you lived your days. And when you hit the hay at night, you settle easy, you sleep the sleep of the just and you can say, 'Take me away.'"
>
> He said, "Harry, all my life I've wanted to be a painter, and I've painted. God, I would have loved to be more successful, but I've painted, and I've painted, and I am 'good tired,' and they can take me away."

Harry finishes by saying, "Now, if there is a process ... that will allow us to live our days, that will allow us that degree of equanimity towards the end, looking at that black implacable wall of death, to allow us that degree of peace, that degree of non-fear, *I want in.*"

My guess is that Harry might have had a few seconds flashing back on his life just before a car accident ended his life. I also like to think that he faced that moment with peace in his soul. He had spent his life devoted to a good cause, not only giving his time and his money but his whole being to helping others.

Harry Chapin and his grandfather remind us that inspired lives are lives worth living. It doesn't matter what you're inspired by—painting, music, feeding the hungry, or serving your family. It only matters that you're inspired and that when you come to the end of your life, you are "good tired" and they can take you away.

The word *inspiration* comes from Latin, and it means "spirit within." You can call that spirit "God" or the "life force" or "Yahweh" or many other names, but we all can see when it's present in the life of someone who lives an inspired life. Seeing the spirit alive inside an inspired person is as easy to see as their face. We all know it when we see it, whether it be Harry Chapin, or people we know personally. Inspired people are lights for all to see.

58. The Hospice

There is a woman named Joyce who is a community activist in Duncan Village, a poor township in East London that is about sixty miles from Open Arms. Joyce lives in the township, and I met her several years ago when she came to Open Arms with a friend to visit one of the children in our care. She is a very tenderhearted person who has great compassion for the suffering of the people around her. Because of that, she loved seeing Open Arms on her initial visit, and we became instant friends.

For the last five or six years, Joyce has served as a tour guide for me and several visitors in Duncan Village. When we have people visit Open Arms, it is always good to have them tour a township so they can see where the children in our care start their lives. Duncan Village probably has a hundred thousand residents, but that could be inaccurate because no one knows how many people live there in the square miles of shacks. It would be impossible to count everyone; there are too many alleyways, too many shacks, too many people coming and going. It was about such a place in Africa that Bono of U2 wrote the famous song "Where the Streets Have No Name." That song is true—the streets and alleyways and footpaths have no names. You just have to know where you're going, and thankfully, Joyce does. She is not a travel guide by trade, but she gives a great tour of the children's homes, neighborhoods, schools, and community centers. She is proud of her community, and given the sheer tenacity of the people who live there, she should be.

In January of 2012, Sallie and I took a group of thirty-three American visitors to Open Arms for the dedication of our new kitchen and dining hall. Many of the travelers on the tour had helped fund the facility and wanted to see the final result of their generosity. It was a wonderful trip.

As in previous years, we scheduled a time for the group to visit Duncan Village. We walked through the neighborhoods, talked with the residents, and saw the plight of the people who live without sewers, water, and electricity. Once you go there, you never forget that you did.

After the tour, as we headed back to the city of East London, Joyce confided in me that her son was in a hospice, very sick with AIDS and tuberculosis. He was in his twenties. She asked if it would be OK for the group to stop at the hospice to visit him. With tears coming down her cheeks, she told me that she wanted her son to know that other people cared about him and were praying for him. My response, also with tears in my eyes, was that it would be a privilege and an honor to visit him. That turned out to be an understatement.

As we stopped and entered the hospice, we saw a female volunteer reading to a child who was on oxygen. HIV/AIDS does not discriminate based on age, and children are just as apt as adults to carry it. It was hard not to be moved by this scene as we walked in the door. It was a stark reminder that we were entering a place with very sick people and, in some cases, very dying ones as well.

Winding down the hallway, all thirty-three of us came to the room where Joyce's son lay in a bed. AIDS is often called "slim" because its sufferers often waste away, and Joyce's son certainly weighed no more than one hundred pounds. Despite his condition, he absolutely beamed as members of our traveling party one by one greeted him and told him that he was in their prayers and thoughts.

It was obvious that this train of well-wishers was making him feel special and loved. More importantly, it was even more special to see Joyce stand in the corner of the room absolutely beaming with a big smile. Her son was the center of attention, and she loved the entire scene as only a mother can. Joyce had been the only visitor that had come to see her son at the hospice, and now there was a busload of them! The son was happy, but his mother was even more overjoyed to see her son receive hug after hug. Needless to say, it was one of many experiences I've had in South Africa that I will never forget.

After the visit was complete, all of us boarded the bus, and Dave Horan, a board member and close friend, hugged me tightly. I am not ashamed to report that we were absolutely sobbing. Certainly, the tears contained sadness at what we had witnessed, but also had joy seeing that we had been able to lift the spirits of one who needed lifting. We had started out feeling intrusive about this visit, entering a hospice to visit a suffering man we didn't even know. We left knowing that we had provided joy to him and his mother, even if temporarily, and it was a privilege to do so. It was also a lasting reminder of the importance of the work we do at Open Arms because, rather bluntly, we often take care of the children of the dead.

Thanks to a heavy dose of HIV medication and other drugs, eventually Joyce's son lived to return home with his mother. Today, his health is not very good, but he continues to battle two enemies in his body with grace and courage. His mother continues to provide the love that only a mother can.

Often in life, we doubt if we can make a difference in the life of another. I don't wonder about that anymore, but if you do, just get in the car to a local nursing home or hospital and erase that doubt from your mind forever. Somewhere close to you, someone is lying in a bed just waiting for a visitor. That life-changing visitor can be you.

59. Heart

Father Stan Rother was a Catholic priest from Oklahoma who worked among dirt-poor Indians in rural Guatemala for thirteen years, from 1968 to 1981. A very humble man, he served the people with incredible dedication, which meant doing just about everything with and for them. He built houses, recharged batteries, visited the sick, dug wells and sewers, hauled trash, married and baptized people, and ministered to his flock in any way he could. He even translated the New Testament and the Catholic mass into the local Tzutuhil language so the locals could fully appreciate the good news of the Gospel. For this, Fr. Rother was loved and admired by thousands of the poor families he served with humility and love.

Father Rother also believed that everyone who died should get a proper funeral and burial. So when Guatemalan military death squads murdered local people in the country's civil war in the 1970s and early '80s, he would go pick up the body, hold a funeral mass, and bury the deceased. The military did not like him doing this, and in 1981 he was sent back home to Oklahoma because his name had been found on the military's death list. After three months in the United States, he appealed to his bishop to return to Guatemala because, he wrote, "My people need me" and "I can't stay away from them any longer."

Stan Rother was allowed to go back to Guatemala in April 1981. In late July of that year, two assassins broke into the church rectory and killed Father Rother by shooting him in the head. He died for the people he served. His killers were never found.

When news about the murder spread among the local townspeople, they all gathered at the church. More than a thousand people stood outside all day praying for their beloved priest. And before Father Rother's body was flown back to Oklahoma for burial, the local people had a rather unusual and yet monumentally beautiful request for his parents: they asked that Fr. Stan's heart be removed first so that it could remain with the people he loved so much. The request was granted, and Stan Rother's heart was buried in the floor of the church where he served God and his people with complete dedication. The rest of Stan was buried back home in Oklahoma.

I have reflected on Father Rother's life many times. The way he lived his life is a wonderful example for the rest of us, which is why the Catholic Church is considering making him a saint. But as Stan Rother and many other people prove, you don't have to be a saint to be an example to others. You just have to live a life that matters.

Reflecting on Father Rother's life, it naturally begs a larger question about our own lives. Where should *our* hearts be buried after we're gone? The local tavern? The country club? Our church? Our workplace? Under our family's house? At the local soup kitchen?

The answer to that question is about as central to our lives as any question can be. Stan Rother's life should challenge us all. Who will fight for our hearts after we're gone? What are we giving our hearts to, and why does it matter?

60. Bert's Buses

Bertha Jensen spent her adult life teaching grade school children in St. Paul, Minnesota. She grew up in Hudson, Wisconsin, and moved west to Minnesota as a young woman. She never married but instead dedicated herself to the important business of educating children in a classroom for more than forty years. She took her job very seriously, and by all reports, she was an excellent teacher. After retiring, Bertha moved to Arizona to enjoy the warmer weather, and she became a client of mine in the mid-1990s.

Many things could be said about Bertha Jensen, but one thing could not: that she was loose with her money. She spent a lifetime saving diligently and bought blue-chip stocks when she could afford them. As a result, she built up a solid foundation for her retirement, supplemented by a teacher's pension earned one semester at time for more than four decades.

Bertha first heard about Open Arms through her nephew, Bill Allds, also a client of mine and a good friend. Upon hearing about the orphanage, she decided it was time to spend some money. She was in her early nineties, and it was the first time she had ever loosened her purse strings. To her everlasting credit, she decided to do it not for herself but for poor children, as if she had not done enough for children already.

One day, Bertha called me and asked me to come visit her at the assisted living place she then called home. As usual, I prepared a review of her portfolio, thinking she would want to go over her investments. When I arrived, she told me to put the papers on the dresser and to sit down to talk about something "more important." She told me that she had decided to do something special for the orphaned children at Open Arms and then asked for a list of needs we had at the time. I told her washing machines were needed. She didn't seem to react. I told her we needed some bunk beds for the kids. Again, not much reaction came from Bertha. I then told her we needed a fourteen-passenger van to get kids to and from school. Her eyes instantly lit up like fireworks on the Fourth of July. "A school bus?" she asked. Yes, I told her we really needed one, but we had priced a new Toyota Quantum at $36,000, far too expensive for a gift from her. She told me that she had worked all her life, and now being in her nineties, she knew she was not going to outlast her money. Just the opposite—it was going to outlast her. With firm resolve, she told me that our first school bus was going to come from her, and there would be no more discussion about it. My first thought was how humbling it was to hear her words. She had saved all her life and now decided to spend some money on someone else.

A few months later, "Bert's Bus" arrived at Open Arms, and we were thrilled to have it. We had grown to house more than twenty children, and the bus was desperately needed to get kids to and from school and other activities. I took a photo of all of the children in front of our wonderful new bus with the words "Bert's Bus" painted on the side. A week later, I presented it to Bertha, and you could tell that she couldn't have been more pleased. A school bus made possible by a schoolteacher. She proudly displayed the photo of children she would never meet in her small room, and I think it gave her great joy.

About a year or so later, I got a call from Bertha to return to see her. Once again, I prepared a review of her investments, and once again, the meeting had nothing to do with that. Bertha had read in our newsletter that we had added a number of children and asked about the bus situation. I told her that we were quickly outgrowing our new van, and that's all she needed to hear. Within a month, "Bert's Bus Too" was in our driveway at Open Arms, courtesy of the woman who ended up spending some of her life savings on someone else's children. Quite sadly, Bertha died within months of making this second gift. But every time we put the key in the ignition of either van, she proves she is still with us in a very important way.

In September 2012, I was traveling with our children at Open Arms to a local town to serve food to people who live at the dump there. I was riding in Bert's Bus, and I saw the Bert's Bus Too decal prominently displayed on the back window of the Open Arms van in front of us. I quickly got my camera out to take a photo from behind the van. I figured I'd send it to Bertha's nephew Bill to remind him of the great things that Bertha continued to make possible. Ten minutes later, we pulled into the dump in the vans that she had been so proud to provide.

As the children and adults came to get food and blankets from our kids, I continued to think about Bertha. Not only were the vans bringing our children to school every day, but now they were engaged in good works of mercy as well. Just as we were finishing up distributing the food, a small boy covered from head to toe in dirt came up to us. I don't think I've ever seen a dirtier child in my life. My heart just melted as I saw him come forward to ask for a sandwich. As he worked through the crowd, I gasped when I saw what he was wearing: a filthy jacket that had one word printed across the chest. The word on the jacket simply said in block letters, "Wisconsin." Here in a dump, more than ten thousand miles from America's Dairyland, came a hungry and filthy child wearing the most unlikely thing imaginable: a Wisconsin jacket, a jacket from Bertha Jensen's home state.

You will never, ever convince me that the poor boy in that dump wasn't a real and tangible reminder of the teacher from Wisconsin who made that trip possible. I had just been thinking about her, and then came the poor youngster in the Wisconsin jacket that proclaimed the schoolteacher from Wisconsin was right there with us as if she had been standing there herself.

After Bertha's death, her nephew Bill told me a poignant story that he had shared with Bertha as she neared death's door. Bill had told Bertha that when she got to the gates of heaven, she should expect to be picked up by an African woman in a shiny new van who was going to say, "Hi Bert, we've been expecting you!" He said that mental picture gave her great comfort.

Bertha Jensen taught thousands of youngsters in the St. Paul school system. But the most important lesson she ever taught was the example of her life.

61. A Child Is Born

The world over, people celebrate the birth of a child with great joy. The family gathers, and the newness of life is embraced and lifted up. There is nothing in life like a newborn baby. It is a cause for great celebration.

At Open Arms, we have received seven children right after they were born. These children have come from parents who could not handle a newborn baby either because they were too young themselves or too desperate in their own circumstances to care for the child. In the latter circumstance, the child is often abandoned right in the hospital and sent to us.

I have learned not to pass judgment on these situations for I have never been a new parent at age fourteen nor too sick or poor to care for myself much less someone else. Instead, I have learned to do what the children and staff at Open Arms do on such occasions: celebrate the arrival of a newborn child and give that child all the love we can. The arrival of a newborn child is cause for great celebration, and it is great to see the joy that a baby brings to our campus. Everyone rushes to see the new arrival and to hold and feed him or her. With more than forty mamas and tatas onsite and more than fifty brothers and sisters, the new child need not worry about a lack of attention. It is coming whether the child is ready or not!

Every child on earth deserves such attention after birth. They deserve to have others celebrate their firsts, whether it's walking or cooing or laughing or rolling over. These milestones should be celebrated for every child regardless of circumstance.

Open Arms exists to serve children from birth through young adulthood. But I'd be lying if I didn't say we have a soft spot for babies. After all, we're just like any other family. We celebrate new life and are privileged to be a part of it. How the children come to us is not nearly as important as the celebration and joy that ensues. Life itself is God's greatest gift, and we are privileged to celebrate the little ones he brings our way, regardless of how it happens.

62. Faith to Move Anthills

Raising funds for charitable activities is as much of the work of a charity as the chartable activity itself. Every single member of our ten-member board of directors works hard to keep our funding on pace with the growth of the children who call Open Arms home. As president of our small organization, I feel this pressure too, especially in light of the difficult economy that makes raising money difficult.

It was particularly challenging for us in 2012. We accepted eleven new children, hired more staff, and we consumed ever larger amounts of electricity, water, gasoline, and food. More children mean more school uniforms and higher tuition costs. Very simply, it costs more to serve more.

In light of this, it is often easy to get discouraged and wish that we had more money than we do. Our donors are very generous; they continually inspire me with their selfless giving and sacrifice on behalf of children whom they will probably never meet. They care deeply about our work, and they prove it every year by helping us move forward. But given the reality of more children at Open Arms, we need more donors both large and small.

My dad used to say that "you can't raise a family on S&H Green Stamps." Those words were spoken by a true child of the Depression who lived his entire childhood in an apartment because his family couldn't afford a house. Remembering those words, I've also learned that you can't raise dozens of children in South Africa on good intentions. It takes money, and that can be challenging for a small organization like ours. We try our best to continue to spread the good news of this ministry through word of mouth and small fundraising events that don't cost much money. It's similar to taking a hill in a war—you usually make progress in inches and sometimes question whether you're making progress at all.

The one thing that seems to make the ultimate difference for us is that God himself is good and gracious. In short, he makes things possible for us when they don't seem possible. The new donor shows up right at the right time, or the large check comes in just when we were scratching our heads about next quarter's budget. I don't think this is coincidental. The book of James says, "Religion that is pure and undefiled before God and the Father is this: to care for orphans and widows in their affliction and to keep one unstained by the world." I take this to mean that God is behind us.

In some ways, 2012 was a discouraging year due to a very tight budget. We needed $35,000 per month to meet our needs. But in other ways, 2012 was encouraging. We are still standing and serving more children than ever.

I don't read scripture as much as I should. Of course, I don't do a lot of things as much as I should (exercise comes to mind). But when I get particularly discouraged about finances at Open Arms, I turn to a passage in the seventeenth chapter of Matthew, where Jesus says, "Amen, I say to you, if you have faith the size of a mustard seed, you will say to this mountain, 'Move from here to there,' and it will move. Nothing will be impossible for you."

On most days, I think my faith is not strong enough to move anthills, much less mountains. But thankfully, God is on the job even when we are not.

It's important to always be on the lookout for more donors and gifts that will help our children. That work never ends. But in the final analysis, it's probably more important to read Matthew 17:20 and know that nothing is impossible if we will only believe.

Move, mountain; move!

63. The River

I believe that God has a plan for each of us, if only we'll take the time to listen to his voice and then obey the voice we hear. For this reason, I often think of God's voice or personal call to us as a river—actually "The River," the source of calling in our lives. The Spirit of God calls everyone to his purpose, and I believe that as human beings we have five possible responses to the presence of The River in our lives.

The first person along The River is the person who stands on the shore and faces into the forest. This person doesn't see The River, doesn't feel The River, and doesn't even perceive it exists, even though it surely does if they'll only turn around. This person instead only focuses on the forest. They don't know the power of The River and its ability to provide life-giving water or to transport them to a better place. It's all about the forest.

To this person, the call of God and his voice are ignored entirely.

The second person along The River is the person who stands on the shore and faces The River. This person spends his or her entire life looking at The River, realizing its potential but never touching it out of fear or ignorance or both. They see how The River might possibly quench their thirst or allow them to get somewhere much faster than they could walk on the shore, but this remains merely a curiosity for their entire lives. They choose to live life on the bank, suspecting that life could offer them more if only they would enter or touch The River. Unlike the person facing into the forest, they see the great power of The River but fear or ignorance keeps them away.

To this person, there is an inkling, an inner urge, to take advantage of a calling that is heard either strongly or faintly. The voice is heard but it is largely ignored.

The third person along The River is the one who sees its power and perceives it has an advantage over standing on the shore. They feel The River has so many advantages that they overcome fear and doubt and they do something the first two people never do—they jump in The River, feeling it to be a better place to be than standing on the shore. An odd thing happens to this third person, however. After jumping in the river, they immediately start to swim against the current. They perceive the power of The River, which is why they jumped into it in the first place. But once they do so, they feel that they are better served by swimming against the current to follow their own agenda, even when others can see their folly and the great effort swimming against the current takes. What's more, because they are swimming upstream, they never really get anywhere.

To this person, the voice of God is heard, but the call of that voice is overcome by a personal agenda or societal pressures. The result is a person who swims in place and makes very little progress, even though the voice was heard and acted upon.

The fourth person along The River is one who sees its power and acts upon it, just like the third person. The difference for this person is that after jumping in, they decide not to swim upstream but to float with the current. This person, unlike the first three people, goes on a grand adventure because they are flowing with the current and get to see the many wondrous things that The River brings as they travel far downstream. What's more, this fourth person uses very little effort because the great current of The River is carrying them along. For this reason, the fourth person can travel great distances and experience wondrous things the previous three persons cannot even imagine. But interestingly enough, this person is also subject to the dangers of large rocks, dangerous rapids, and waterfalls that often lie downstream. After all, surrendering to the current of the river brings danger along with opportunity. Their decision to merely float with the current brings great adventure but has its share of danger too.

To this person, the voice of God is heard and the call is obeyed too. This surrender allows The River to carry the person to places the first three persons can only dream of. However, their decision to merely float down The River makes them subject to its dangers. Letting The River take them downstream ensures a great adventure, but it does not preclude danger or freedom from pain.

The fifth person along The River is the person who perceives its power, jumps in, and decides to swim along with the current. This person can travel the farthest distance of all because they harness the power of The River along with the energy they themselves can create. Like the fourth person, they are subject to the dangers downstream, but they do a better job of avoiding such dangers because they are swimming to avoid them. This fifth person has an experience that no one else has: they travel farther and see more things than the others. They take full advantage of The River and their own ability to swim with the current. They go on a grand adventure and avoid many of the dangers of the fourth person.

To this last person, the voice of God is heard and obeyed, and they work with all their strength to make sure the call is carried out. This person hears the call, surrenders his or her own agenda, acts on the call, and then works tirelessly to carry it out. This fifth person often becomes one with The River and not only hears the call but carries it out with great effectiveness.

At different times in our lives, each of us can represent one of the five people in the story of The River. Sometimes we are looking in the forest, and other times we are swimming against the current, sure that our own personal agenda is best. Other times, we surrender to the current—and we might even swim with it.

Looking at some of the greatest people of the past century, we often see that they derived their power by being the fifth person in the analogy. People like Gandhi, Nelson Mandela, and Mother Teresa all heard the call of The River, listened to its voice, and then did everything they could to act on it. These people impacted not only those around them but the entire world. In fact, for most of their lives, they spoke and acted as if The River flowed right through them.

One doesn't have to be world famous to be the fifth person in the story of The River. One only has to hear the voice, obey it without hesitation, and then work as if everything depended on it, because everything most surely does.

64. If You Want to Walk on Water

When Sallie and I were contemplating whether to start Open
Arms, I read a book written by John Ortberg called *If You Want
to Walk on Water, You've Got to Get Out of the Boat.* Ortberg is
a Christian pastor, and I have read all of his books. They are
provocative, funny and insightful. *If You Want to Walk on Water* is
my favorite Ortberg book.

In the Gospels, there is a story about the disciples being on a
boat on the Sea of Galilee in the middle of a tremendous storm. Jesus
is not with them, having stayed on the shore to pray. The disciples
are fearful for their lives, sure the boat is going to capsize and they
are all going to drown. If you have ever been on a lake or the ocean
when a storm hits, you know how terrifying that can be. There is
simply no place to hide.

In the midst of the storm, the disciples see what they think is a
ghost on the water and cry out in fear. But the figure is not a ghost—
it is Jesus coming out to them, walking on water and reassuring them
to not be afraid because he is with them. This narrative takes place
in the three Gospels of Mark, Luke, and Matthew, but interestingly
Matthew adds an additional twist not recorded in the other two.

In Matthew, after Jesus reassures the terrified disciples, the
disciple Peter calls out to Jesus and says, "Lord, if it is you, command

me to come to you on the water." Jesus then says, "Come," and Peter gets out of the boat and starts walking toward Jesus. But Matthew writes that after a while, Peter "saw the wind," meaning he realized how bad the conditions were. He began to sink and asked Jesus to save him from drowning. Jesus helps Peter to the boat and says "You of little faith, why did you doubt?"

There are many angles to this amazing story, and Ortberg covers them in great detail in the book. He writes about how doubts can cause a person to sink and also about how Jesus will always be with us in the storms of our life. But Ortberg makes two points about the story that really had a profound impact on me and led in part to the founding of Open Arms.

First, because of his faith, Peter became the second and only human being in recorded history to actually walk on water! This is significant because after Christ commanded him to get out of the boat, Peter actually did. He accomplished something that has not been accomplished since: he walked on the surface of water—in a storm no less!

The point that Ortberg so brilliantly makes is that if we too want to walk on water, we too have to get out of the boat. Stated differently, if we want to accomplish great things in our lives, we have to face our fears and actually get out of our comfort zone ("the boat"). This means placing our faith in God and actually doing things that we might never be able to accomplish on our own. It is faith that allows this to happen, and Peter's walk across the Sea of Galilee in a storm is a great example of what is possible if we obey God's call and place our fears aside.

Ortberg goes onto to also examine a point I had not previously considered when reading the story. He talks about the other disciples in the boat and how they must have always regretted not having Peter's bold faith. While Peter listened to Jesus's call and accomplished something great, they just sat there and watched. Ortberg calls the other disciples "boat potatoes" and laments their lack of faith and, just as importantly, their lack of action. Only Peter accomplished a walk across water because only Peter had the bold faith to step out of the boat when God called him.

We all have fears that hold us back from accomplishing something wonderful for God. Our fear may be of failing, or spending money we could use for other purposes, or just looking foolish to those around us. But as the fourteenth chapter of the Gospel of Matthew shows us, sitting in our comfort zone and fearing for our lives not only makes us look cowardly but prevents us from feeling the exhilaration of actually doing something that only faith can make possible.

If we want to walk on water, we surely must get out of the boat. An exhilarating experience may be just on the other side of our fears, and God is calling us to walk with him, even on a stormy lake. Boat potatoes we cannot be.

65. Service Above Self

There is an organization that has 1.3 million members and meets in 33,000 locations around the world every week. Its members gather not to further a political or religious agenda but merely to do good for others. The organization does simple things like feed the homeless and give dictionaries to low-income students and wheelchairs to people who previously crawled in the dirt to get around. It also does complicated things like leading the charge to rid the world of the scourge of polio (an objective that is almost fulfilled). In exchange for their service, the members of this organization are paid absolutely nothing and give so freely of themselves that it's no surprise to anyone that their motto consists of three simple words: "Service Above Self."

The organization that is making such a difference in the world is called Rotary, and I have been proud to call myself a member since 2007. That year, a friend of mine, Shari Hargrave, asked me to join the Sun City Rotary Club. To be honest, I didn't know how to say no, so I just showed up and said I'd join. It was one of the best decisions I have made.

They often say there is a time lapse between the date a person joins Rotary and the day they truly become a Rotarian. A good friend of mine and Sun City Rotary member, Jim Green, once said that the time lapse for him was several years. He had joined Rotary to make business contacts and quickly found out people there were not necessarily interested in making money through Rotary. Quite the opposite—they were more interested in giving it away.

In 2002, Jim decided to go to the annual worldwide gathering of Rotarians at their international conference. That year, the conference was held in Barcelona, Spain. Jim described the opening scene of the gathering, which was held in a large arena. On the stage in the building was a single chair lit by a spotlight. A man came out onto the stage and started doing somersaults and tumbling exercises to African music. After the music ended, Jim said the man walked over to the chair, sat down, and promptly removed his legs. He then told the crowd that his legs had been given to him by Rotary. It was at that instant, Jim told me, that he actually became a member of the organization that he had joined years before. Jim has gone on to do great things in Rotary, including serving as our district governor a few years back.

I became a Rotarian in 2007 after Shari asked me to join. I quickly began to appreciate the fellowship and good works of my Club in Sun City. We have thirty members, and like every Rotary Club, we like to have fun, raise money, and give it all away. In my first year, I enjoyed getting to know people and doing good works, but I can't really say that I was truly a committed Rotarian. That all changed the following year.

In 2008, Open Arms was out of space. We had grown to provide a home for thirty children, and we had no room to accept more. Because of the overwhelming need for homes for orphaned children in South Africa, it is very hard to consistently say no when the local authorities call to ask if we can take more kids. For that reason, our organization decided to do something that would give us the opportunity to say yes again. It was time for me to hit the road.

In August of 2008, I embarked on a 710-mile walk across South Africa to raise money for four additional cottages at Open Arms. Called "A Long Walk for Children," the effort was an attempt to raise awareness and funds that would allow us to increase our capacity again.

Knowing that I would walk through a number of South African towns on the way, I contacted the East London Sunrise Rotary Club to inquire if they would be willing to assist with logistical help on the walk across the country. A man named John Roberts immediately responded to my call for help and said that they would be glad to assist the effort. Such a response is typical of most Rotarians; they say yes to other Rotarians' pleas for assistance, even if they don't know them personally. They instinctively figure that any Rotarian is a good person, and I personally know of no instance where they are not right to assume this.

John quickly followed up his first email with another that indicated he had contacted Rotary Clubs along the planned route for the walk, and he once again reported they would all be happy to help. And so, Rotary Clubs in places that I only knew on a map— East London, Grahamstown, Port Elizabeth, Plettenberg Bay, Jeffries Bay, Knysna, Swellendam, and Somerset West—decided that they would host me and my two traveling companions when we walked through their area. They said they would provide logistical support, housing, food, and whatever other service they could provide as we traversed on foot across the country. Mind you, these people were complete strangers to me. I only knew they were Rotarians, and the only thing they knew about me was the same. Apparently, my membership in Rotary was the only background check they needed.

As we traversed the country, the Rotarians I met went above and beyond the call of duty, welcoming us like we were long-lost relatives. They fed us, welcomed us to their clubs, housed us in their homes, washed our clothes, recommended doctors and auto mechanics, and provided help to us in every way possible. We walked into each town as strangers, and a few days later, we left as good friends. Little did those kindhearted people know, they were teaching me what it truly meant to be a Rotarian. Just like my friend Jim Green, I ended up becoming a Rotarian not on the day of my induction but after having an experience that truly showed the value of the organization. Jim's breakthrough moment came when watching a man dance on life-giving artificial legs; mine came when I used my real legs to walk into the homes of some of the most generous and giving people you will find anywhere.

This week, like every week, 1.3 million people will gather in communities around the world with just one aim: to serve humanity with no thought of reward. These people will hold fundraising events, fine each other for wearing bad ties to raise money, laugh a lot, and most importantly, plan their next moves to serve humanity. No one will get paid a dime, but every single member will be paid in a far more lasting way—with the satisfaction that comes from putting someone else's needs ahead of their own.

The Rotary motto of "Service Above Self" consists of just three words. You might say these words inspire Rotarians the world over. From my vantage point, I think the words are more far more descriptive than inspirational. They simply describe how Rotarians live their lives. I know this because I have seen it for myself in so many ways, most notably in my own club and on the long road to Cape Town.

I am proud to be a member of Rotary but even more proud to actually be a Rotarian. I will be both for the rest of my life.

66. A Letter from Bobo, Spring 2012

In late January, we hosted a celebration to dedicate our new kitchen and dining facility at Open Arms. It was a great day and featured a marching band, native dancers, thirty-three visitors from the United States, performances by the children, and a big *braai* (a South African barbeque). It was certainly a day to remember and marked a new milestone as we expand our services to more children in the years ahead.

We named our new facility Emmanuel Hall because the word "Emmanuel" in Hebrew and Greek means "God is with us." You may think it is presumptuous of us to claim that "God is with us," but we certainly know it is true! I want to clarify this statement just a bit.

We do not feel "God is with us" because he favors us more than other nonprofit organizations. There are countless nonprofits all over the world performing valuable service. Open Arms is just one of them. We also don't believe that "God is with us" because he favors our children more than any others. We know God loves all children equally. Rather, the reason we know that "God is with us" is because he continually sends us caring and generous people like you who make this ministry possible. Good-hearted people of all faiths continue to step forward to help our children. Simply stated, we know that the word "Emmanuel" is true for us because of you. Your generosity makes our service to children possible.

There is a story of a man who once stood before God complaining of all the pain and suffering in the world. The man asked God why he didn't send some more help. God simply replied, "I did send help. I sent *you.*"

Every day, I am grateful beyond words for the way that you prove that despite appearances, children who have lost their parents are not alone. That is a very powerful message, and it says so much not only about Open Arms but also about you.

As we take in more children in the year ahead, I hope that you will make it possible for our operating budget to grow to meet the demands that serving more children will require. I have no doubt that you will. We have taken in seven new children since January and now have forty-eight kids who call us home.

God is good and very present to us. Every day, we are thankful that he sent us you!

67. Uncle John

Open Arms has been the beneficiary of the work and generosity of many people. One of the most passionate advocates in our short history was John Freese, the brother of my best friend and board member, Ted Freese. In July 2013, John died of cancer at age sixty, and I was asked to share a few words at his memorial service. It was a great privilege to do so, and I am happy to honor John by including the eulogy here. John is very sorely missed by me and so many others, including the entire Open Arms family.

My name is Bob Solis, and I had the privilege of knowing John Freese for more than thirty-five years. John's younger brother Ted has been my best friend since we moved next door to the Freese family in Minnetonka in the spring of 1977. John and I both had hair at the time.

Having been an unofficial member of the Freese family for more than three decades, I have been to my share of weddings, baptisms, Christmas gatherings, birthday parties, and sadly, funerals too. At each of those occasions, I always talked with John. Like all of you, I found him to be funny, thoughtful, a bit crusty, and most of all, a really good guy. John was very well-read, and his often unique perspective on things made it a treat to talk to him. I often thought of John as "the loveable curmudgeon," and it's a title he probably would have liked.

In 2006, my wife Sallie and I started an orphanage in South Africa called Open Arms Home for Children. Being my second family, the Freeses rallied to the cause and became donors and advocates for the orphaned children who came to our doors. When John's sister Ellen died five years ago, she directed that her memorial gifts be given to Open Arms. We took that money and decided to build an amphitheater, an outdoor gathering spot, in Ellen's honor. It was designed to be a place where people could gather to enjoy the view of the valley below and share a laugh or a conversation. It seemed a fitting tribute to Ellen.

In January 2010, John traveled to South Africa to attend a ceremony dedicating four new cottages and Ellen's amphitheater. Family was incredibly important to John, and he wanted to honor his sister by attending the dedication. To say that the trip changed his life would be a great understatement.

On that trip, John's eyes and, more keenly, his heart were opened to the importance of providing a home to children who simply had no other place to go. He hugged and played with the kids, walked through the slums where they came from, made friends with the locals over bonfires and more than few glasses of scotch, and came home on fire about helping the children who would come to affectionately call him "Uncle John."

Now, I won't say John's reaction puzzled me. After all, I always knew him to be a loveable curmudgeon, with the emphasis on loveable. The true love of John's life, his wife Helen, lost both of her parents at a very early age, so maybe he saw an extension of Helen's life in the children at Open Arms. Or maybe it was his great love for his sons Dan and Tom that fired his compassion for children who didn't have parents. Regardless of the reason, that trip to South Africa changed John's life forever. He became a passionate advocate of our children and our ministry. If you worked with him, you know how much he talked about Open Arms. If you are a friend, you know that he spent at least a week every year going to the home to visit "his" kids. If you serve on the Board of Open Arms, then you know how much John and Helen generously donated each year to ensure the kids had the most loving and uplifting home possible. In short, Open Arms added a passion to John's life that brought him joy, meaning, and fulfillment. He carried that passion with him to his final day, when my wife Sallie visited him in the hospital and he thanked her for what he called "the absolute privilege" of being involved in the children's lives. Little did he realize, the privilege was all ours. John was a shining light to our children and staff and to me personally. He will be greatly missed not only here in Minnesota but also on a tiny hilltop in South Africa where his legacy lives on in the lives of children who owe him so much.

In March of 2011, John took a week to go on his annual visit to Open Arms. During that week, one of our children, a tiny two-month-old girl, was struggling with her health. The girl was named Sisana, and she had come to Open Arms at four weeks of age with her twin sister. Both of the girls were in poor health and underweight; they weighed about four pounds each. During John's visit, Sisana was having severe respiratory problems and needed daily visits to the local clinic. John took her. He always wanted to be useful at Open Arms—and he always was. Every day that week, he took her to the clinic, usually waiting for hours to see the doctor with a fussy infant in his lap. Like all things related to Open Arms, John was up to the task. Sisana needed him, and he was happy to be needed. But it had to be a rather odd sight—here was this large, white, middle-aged American man holding a tiny black infant, rocking her back and forth, and telling her that everything would be OK. Rumor has it that the locals who usually see women take children to the clinic took to the unusual sight by calling John "the white mama," and I think he was proud of that title too. I must admit that I still chuckle at that—John Freese, the white mama.

Late in the week of John's visit, it became clear little Sisana was beginning to struggle for her life. We put her into the hospital, and quite tragically, two days later she died only eighty days into her short life. John went to the hospital and helped identify her body, a story he first told me about with tears in his eyes.

I don't know why some people like Sisana are taken away too soon at eighty days of age. I also don't know why John was taken away from us far too soon at age sixty. But I do take great comfort that when John arrived in heaven, he was greeted by his dad, T. E., and his siblings Ellen and Andy, and after those hugs, he turned to see a little South African girl wildly running up to him with her arms wide open, screaming, "Uncle John, where have you been? No one ever took better care of me than you."

68. Travel

One of the essential characteristics of human beings is our tendency to assume that everyone lives like we do. We project our own beliefs and lifestyle onto others, even if we don't know them. For example, we have a house, so too does most everyone else. We have toilets; doesn't everyone?

Overseas travel can put a lot of these assumptions to the test. Suddenly, we learn that a lot of people crap in a pot in the corner of their one-room house. A flush toilet is a dream for them. Or we find that the concept of a "vacation" is unknown. How can you go on vacation if you're just looking for money for the next meal? Watching the ball game on TV? Forget it—you need electricity for that, never mind a TV.

The term *third world* was coined by a French anthropologist in 1952. It was used to describe those countries that were neither aligned with the free nations of the West nor the communist Soviet bloc countries. The term then came to have a pejorative connotation for backward, struggling countries that didn't contribute much to the global economy. After all, it's hard to contribute when all you're trying to do is survive.

If you travel to such areas, you will see people running to work on the side of the road—literally running to a job that pays them a buck or two a day. They return home each night to a shack with no running water or plumbing. They may believe in God, in democracy, in the goodness of the United States. They may not. But their sheer tenacity, their optimism in the face of crushing poverty, can teach us a lot about how much we take for granted.

I have nothing to complain about. I used to, but that was before I traveled overseas. Apparently, billions of people don't live like us.

69. Time Is Not on Our Side, Ever

Most of our lives seem to go by in just a blink of an eye. If we're lucky, we get seventy or eighty years on earth. That may seem like a long time, but life is just like a roll of toilet paper—the more you use it, the faster it goes. I remember when I was in grade school, it seemed like it took four years for Christmas vacation to come around. Now that I've lived fifty years, it seems that every other week it's New Year's Eve again. When I was ten, a year comprised 10 percent of my life. Now, 365 days make up just 2 percent of my time on earth. No wonder life seems to go faster these days.

I can remember a lot of details of my life at age fifteen. That was thirty-eight years ago. If you fast forward thirty-eight years from today, the averages say I will be dead. Some might see that as depressing or stark, but I don't find it so. I find it motivating. The fact that I will be dead soon is a proverbial kick in the rear. Why put off something until tomorrow when tomorrow may never come? It seems silly to wait for golden years to do things that are important. Certainly, opening up an orphanage with five kids coming up on college might have been considered stupid timing. But if we had waited, then what would have happened to dozens of children who needed a home as soon as possible? Our comfort in waiting for the exact right moment to start this project would have caused incredible discomfort to children needing a home right now. Dreams cannot wait. There is simply is no time like today.

In 2008, a man named Dave Freeman fell in his home in Los Angeles, hit his head, and died. This kind of thing is not that uncommon, but it made the news across the country. It made the news because of Freeman's personal history. In 1999, Freeman and a friend wrote a book called *100 Things to Do Before You Die*. In the book, they urged readers to do things like make a voodoo pilgrimage to Haiti, run with the bulls in Pamplona, or have ninety-eight other unforgettable experiences. Apparently, when Freeman died at age forty-seven several years after writing the book, he had done about half of the things on his list.

I didn't find the irony of Freeman's unlived experiences to be tragic. After all, he did fifty things most of us will never do. But to try to do one hundred things before death I think might miss the point. Frankly, we all have some things on our bucket list, but I think it's more important to focus on the two or three things that will define us before we die. Maybe that's being a great parent, a good friend, or volunteer of the year at a local charity. A trip to Stonehenge or to see the Galapagos Islands can be important, but those things will not define us. Regardless of what's on our bucket list, we all are racing a clock that will stop ticking much sooner than we think. That's the reality, and it shouldn't scare us but rather kick us in the rear end.

"Life is a short journey," wrote Freeman in his introduction to his book. He urged the reader to "get off your butt and create a fabulous memory or two" before it was over. I think that's good advice. Dave Freeman died far too young at forty-seven. For those of us who have already lived past forty-seven, what's our excuse? If we don't hear a clock ticking, we simply aren't listening.

70. A Letter from Bobo, Fall 2012

Often in a magazine, you will see an ad for a diet pill or program that shows "before" and "after" photos. The "before" photo is typically a bit fuzzy and is taken from a most unflattering angle. The "after" picture is usually better in every way and attempts to get consumers to believe in the magic of the diet pill or program. Looking at such photos, I often think that it's more important to hire the right photographer than to actually lose weight.

At Open Arms Home, we receive children who usually come to us with just the shirts on their backs. They bring no photos with them, but if they did, their "before" pictures would often be hard to look at. They might show a child suffering in a shack with a very sick or very absent parent. They probably would show a child with no shoes and little food. This would be the reality we would see in the "before" photos, if we had them.

Open Arms Home exists because of these "before" situations, but that is not what we are about. As a small organization working in the midst of great poverty and an AIDS pandemic, we cannot do a lot about the "before" that often makes our children alone in the world. But we can—and we do—focus on the "after." We can control that, and it drives us every day to provide the most loving and uplifting home we can. Your support makes that possible.

Many times I have been told by people that the photos of the children at Open Arms are among the most joyous and beautiful photos that they see. I always love to hear that because our children truly are happy, and I'm glad it comes out in the photos we take of them. Because I take a lot of the photos myself, I know that the "after" photos have nothing to do with the quality of the photographer but rather the joy of the child being photographed. That's what makes our "after" photos different and much more meaningful than diet ads.

A few weeks ago, on September 21, 2012, two eighteen-month-old twin boys came to probably live the rest of their childhood at Open Arms Home for Children. Like all of our children, the boys had endured a very difficult "before" story. Prior to coming to us, they had been in the hospital, one with pneumonia and the other with tuberculosis. During their hospital stay, they were abandoned by a mother who simply left town.

These boys have a special place in our brief history because they are the fiftieth and fifty-first children who now call Open Arms home. Having more than fifty children for the first time is a milestone for us. It means we have a lot of lives to nurture and a lot of responsibility ahead. It means we have to raise more money than ever before. But most importantly, it means that we have to work harder than ever to ensure that the boys' "after" is a lot better than their "before." With your help, I know we will accomplish that goal.

Thank you for making our children's "after" photos so different from their "before" photos. That is why we exist, and it is also why we thank God for you every single day.

71. You Never Know

Prior to buying the land for Open Arms, I went on a trip to the city of Durban to see a few children's homes. While there, I was referred to a Zulu chief who was interested in hearing about our plans for a children's home. He was a man of great power in his community, and I thought it might be good to meet him. He knew that HIV/AIDS was ravaging his people, and he was interested in learning more about the possibility of partnering with us to establish a home for orphans.

Durban is a seaside community, and it is the most tropical big city in South Africa. There are palm trees everywhere and beautiful beaches on the Indian Ocean. Being so tropical, the summer is hot and humid. It certainly was the day I was introduced to the chief.

We drove to a very hilly neighborhood full of *rondavels*, the circular thatched-roof huts that are typical for such communities. The floors are made of hardened dung, but there is no odor. The door to the hut was only about five feet tall, so I had to bend down quite a bit to get inside. As I entered, I was introduced to the chief and about six or seven of his deputies. They all had long pants on and no shirts due to the heat and humidity. The chief obviously ate very well and had a very large and protruding belly. No one in the hut spoke any English, so I spoke to the chief through a man who had accompanied me for the visit. The chief welcomed me and then asked me why I had come to see him. As I began to tell him our plans to open a home for orphaned children, he interrupted me after about twenty seconds. He began to speak for about ten minutes in Zulu to his assembled council. While he did this, they passed around a large wooden bowl of beer that they all shared and replenished a couple of times. I was not offered any beer as the bowl passed by me a couple of times. I did not mind at all.

As the chief went on and on, I could hardly control myself from bursting out with laughter. I had great respect for the chief and the Zulu culture—the comedy of the situation had nothing to do with that. Rather, it was an almost out-of-body experience, one of those settings you find utterly strange only because you are a part of it. Here I was, a guy who grew up in suburban Minneapolis, sitting in a hot circular hut with seven guys with no shirts. They had asked me to meet their leader and then allowed me to speak for about twenty seconds before they got into a heated debate while they drank beer from a common bowl. Try as I might, I could not help but keep looking at the door for a movie camera to show up. The whole scene seemed like it was out of a goofy Jim Carrey movie except that I was a part of it.

After a ten-minute discussion that seemed heated at times, the chief turned to me and, through an interpreter, told me that while they thought our plans were admirable, they would only accept our money to build a children's home. We would have no input on its construction or operation. I respectfully thanked the chief for his time and told him I would consider his offer. I shook everyone's hand and headed to the car to hopefully find a working air conditioner.

Life brings us many unexpected experiences. Anyone who has lived for any amount of time knows that. But personally, I never thought it would bring a boy from Minnetonka, Minnesota, to a meeting with a very large and bare-chested Zulu chief who drank beer from a bowl and then gave me all of twenty seconds to explain a project to him. I probably will never meet a chief again, but my first meeting created a memory that will last a lifetime. I still chuckle when I think about it. Anything—yes, anything—is possible in this life.

72. American Eyes

....

It's been said that "we do not see the world as it is, but we see the world as we are." This is an extremely accurate saying in my opinion, and it very much applies to visitors to another culture, especially if they are American.

One of the difficulties for American visitors to any other culture is that while we leave our country physically, we do not leave our country mentally. It is understandable why we do this; we've been trained to look at the world in a certain way, and it's hard to lose that perspective just because we go on a two-week vacation. This is true for non-Americans too, but since the United States dominates so much of the world economically, militarily, and culturally, I think we tend to see the world with our own eyes more than others do. For example, our military has a physical presence in more than one hundred countries around the world—no other country is even close. We send our soldiers to these faraway places to protect our interests, to save people from themselves, or to bring our way of life to those who we perceive need it. This attitude has done a lot of good in the world, but it carries with it a very real danger of thinking that the way we think is the right way to think. If only people in France or the Congo or Vietnam or Mexico would just come around to our way of thinking and doing, they just might get it right. This kind of thinking can be very dangerous and often leads to disastrous consequences.

I am an American. I am proud of that in so many ways. But I cannot let that stand in the way of going humbly to another place or culture and finding the strengths of that place and people even though it is far different than what I have experienced living in the suburbs of cities in America.

When recent college graduates come to serve as year-long volunteers at Open Arms, I send usually send them a thank you card and a quote before they arrive. The quote is from the late Max Warren, an Anglican missionary leader, who wrote, "Our first task whenever approaching another people, another culture, another religion, is to take off our shoes for the place we are approaching is holy. Else we may find ourselves treading on people's dreams. More serious still, we may forget that God was here before our arrival."

I carry this quote in my wallet. Whenever I land in South Africa on a trip to Open Arms, I take it out and read it. I pray that God will allow me to see his hand in whatever I see and whomever I meet. I ask that he will allow me to be a gracious guest in a culture that is not my own.

The Xhosa culture, just like my American one, has many facets, and there is much to be learned from it. God has been with the Xhosa people in South Africa well before I arrived and he will be with them long after I am gone. Try as I might, I cannot completely take off my American eyes and remove my American brain and set them on the nightstand until I return home. But I try to do this as best I can.

Humility is not a striking American trait, but it will never be unless we try to make it so.

73. God Is With Us

Today is Christmas day. It is the seventh Christmas we've celebrated at Open Arms. The day has special significance for Christians everywhere because we celebrate the day that God became man in the form of Jesus Christ. In announcing the birth to Mary, Jesus's mother, the angel Gabriel tells the mother-to-be that her son will be called Emmanuel, which means "God is with us." This same name had been foretold centuries before by the prophet Isaiah.

I have long felt that the word "Emmanuel" is the sweetest word in the Bible or in any human language. For human beings who often suffer, who often question, who often feel lonely, the word Emmanuel, "God is with us," is the most important word there can be. "Emmanuel" not only means that "God is with us" but it also implies that we are worth being with, that we are worth being saved. What's more, the birth of Christ implies that God is not some far-off, impersonal being but one that understands us, who actually knows what it's like to be human. He knows what it's like be hungry and tempted and tired and frustrated and to suffer. Jesus experienced all of these things, and he still found us sinners loveable, ultimately loveable, just the same.

For children who have lost their families at a young age, I think that the word "Emmanuel" holds even more special meaning, even if the children can't articulate it. When children find themselves all alone in the world, they cherish anything that makes them feel like a part of something. A God that will never abandon us holds special meaning for children who find themselves abandoned or orphaned.

The birth of Jesus reminds us that no matter what happens in our life, God is with us. It's the essential message of Christmas, even if we distract ourselves with gifts, parties, and cards. For children in need, it's a message that holds special significance. No matter how alone they feel, God is with them. And he is with us too.

Christmas, the celebration of Emmanuel, means God is with orphaned children. It also means he is with billionaires, the homeless, with presidents and prime ministers, with janitors, celebrities, and bus drivers. He is with black people and white people and everyone in between. He is with the healthiest athletes and those with terminal illnesses. He is with a child born today and an old woman spending her last day on earth.

This is what we celebrate on Christmas. God is among us, knows what we go through, and loves us in spite of everything we often do to push him out of our lives.

The word gospel means "good news." And the good news, the best news, is that God as Emmanuel has become one of us and he is with us forever. How could any word in any language mean more?

74. The Why

··

Lots of people ask me how Open Arms started. They are naturally curious about how a family of seven in Phoenix, Arizona, started a home for orphaned children on the other side of the world. I have told the story of how we got started many times in talks about the home; it's an important part of our organization's history. How we got started is interesting, I suppose, because it's an unusual story. "Middle-class family in Arizona starts orphanage project in Africa" could be the headline. But nine years into our history, the how question has lost a lot of relevance now that we have fifty-seven children and a $700,000 annual budget. After all, the "how we began" story doesn't pay the bills nor does it make a difference to the children we serve; they just want a place to live and feel loved.

The far more important question about Open Arms is not the how question, it's the why question. *Why* did we get started? *Why* does Open Arms exist? *How* is an interesting question, but *why* gets to the core of our mission. And interestingly enough, the question hardly ever gets asked. And not only does the question not get asked but Sallie and I hardly asked it *ourselves* when we decided to take all of our money and give it away in 2005.

Thankfully, I have had nine years to reflect on that question. It's an important one to ponder, not only to put the past nine years into perspective but hopefully the next ninety years of our organization's existence. But first, we should eliminate a few whys that might be obvious but untrue.

According to World Vision, there are currently more than 17 million AIDS orphans in the world. These children suffer greatly. They need a place to call home. But that is not why Open Arms Home for Children exists. Sallie and I did not wake up one morning and decide that orphaned children needed to be given a home, much less by us and our friends. That would be a very odd thing for a couple with five kids of their own to raise. And frankly, it didn't happen that way.

Sallie and I have attended church with our families since birth. We are Catholic Christians and have heard for as long as we can remember about how we all have a responsibility to take care of those in need. We have always tried to take that responsibility seriously. It's one of the reasons that we took two children into our family twenty years ago. But to claim that our Christian duty made it obvious that we needed to found Open Arms is also a falsehood. It may have contributed to our decision, but it certainly did not serve as the main "why" behind the project.

And finally, one might think that we started Open Arms because we have always had a soft spot in our hearts for children. While that is true, the goal of saving children's lives or being of service to them was not the main driving force in the creation of this project. Those are lofty and admirable goals, but they were not our primary motivation.

Rather, the genesis—the why of Open Arms—was really inspired by something much more simple. The home was not founded because of lofty goals or extraordinary vision or Christian virtue. Rather it was founded because of the existence of fourteen people, twelve of whom were alive in 2006 when the home began and two that were dead. It was people who provided the why, and the people were members of our family: Bill and Lou Ann (my late parents); Eddie and Hope (Sallie's parents); my brothers, Bill and Tom; Sallie's siblings, Sandra, Alicia, and Eddie; and our five children, Alicia, Jaala, Lou Ann, Sammy, and Jonsy.

The why behind Open Arms can be summed up with one word: family. In our case, that family spanned three generations. The first, or older generation, consisted of our parents. Sallie and I grew up in wonderful families with fantastic parents. Our parents were not perfect—far from it. But they loved their children and proved it every single day. They came to all the ball games, plays, doctor's appointments, and parent-teacher conferences (which weren't always good for Sallie or me). More importantly, they provided tender love often and the tougher version when that was needed too. They gave us love and security and the confidence to go into the world as young people with the requisite roots and wings that we all need to thrive.

The next generation that provided the why for Open Arms was our siblings. Sallie and I are blessed with incredible siblings that remain very close to us to this day. Our brothers and sisters are responsible for the greatest laughs we have ever had, the fun of being uncles and aunts, and that deep, lifelong bond that only siblings can provide. When your brothers and sisters bring you so much joy, you wish everyone had people in their lives like Bill and Tom, and Sandra, Alicia, and Eddie. People often say that close friends are like "sisters or brothers." That is a very high compliment when you have siblings like we do.

Ultimately, the main reason for Open Arms consisted of our five children. Our children, plain and simple, have provided the greatest joy in our lives. They have provided the bulk of the laughter, joy, smiles, and satisfaction that we have felt in the last thirty years. Like our parents, they are not perfect either. But they are perfect for us.

When you have the great gift of family, you realize it is the very best thing that life has to offer. There is no substitute in life for having people around you that love you *no matter what*. When you have that, you realize that almost anything is possible. When you don't have it, life loses a lot of its richness and you begin to believe that most things are simply out of your reach.

When we traveled with our children to South Africa in 2004, we saw so many orphaned children who were hurting. Our faith, our position of privilege as Americans, and our love for children all contributed to the idea that Open Arms could become a reality. But it actually became a reality because of our family. We loved our family so much that we couldn't bear the thought of children not having one, even if it wasn't the one they were born into.

There is a wall in the main house at Open Arms that is painted with the words: "There are lots of different ways to make a family. It just takes love. Share your home and share your heart." I don't know which one of our volunteers painted that saying. I don't know if they just made the saying up. But the words on that wall convey a fundamental truth: family is one of the greatest gifts God gives us, and those who have a good one know it. At Open Arms, that truth is written on the wall and, more critically, in the hearts of children who know the joy created by a large family rooted in love.

Family—both having one and wanting to create one—is the reason Open Arms exists. To us, that's a lot more meaningful than the story of how it started. It is about sharing a great gift that you wish all people could have, especially children who are all alone.

75. A Letter from Bobo, Spring 2010

What a start to the year! On January 30, we dedicated four new cottages and our beautiful new amphitheater. We were very pleased to have nineteen visitors from America with us in addition to more than two hundred local folks who joined us for a big day to remember. The big celebration included a marching band, native dancers, readings from our kids, and speeches from local dignitaries. The ceremonies were followed by a delicious BBQ dinner that featured lamb and pork on a spit. A great time was had by all!

As pleased as I was with the celebration, I was even more pleased two days later when we welcomed our first new child in more than a year. Three-year-old Thandaza was welcomed to Open Arms on February 1. Her mother is dying of AIDS and tuberculosis in the hospital, and she had no place else to go.

Thandaza is very underweight for her age. She has obviously been malnourished, probably due to her mother's weakened condition. Thankfully, Thandaza tested negative for HIV/AIDS.

When I look at Thandaza, I see a young child who has lived through a very difficult period in her life. But I am thankful every day that she is now home. We look forward to fattening her up on good food and giving her the love that every child deserves.

I know Thandaza's photo will look very different a year from now. But the sparkle in her eyes even today tells me of the great possibilities ahead.

Children like Thandaza are the reason that Open Arms exists. And as we get ready to welcome more children soon, she is the surest proof that your support is changing lives. What a blessing you are to this child and to all our kids!

76. South Bend

In our third year of operation at Open Arms, it became clear that we needed additional help educating our children. Because of the difficult situations that our children come from, they are often behind educationally and need extra help with homework and tutoring to catch up. To meet this need, we decided to recruit recent college graduates to serve our children, offering them a round trip to South Africa as the only payment they would receive. Naturally, having graduated from Notre Dame myself, we turned to my alma mater to establish a postgraduate program. It has been one of the wisest decisions we have made since we opened our doors.

Every February, I fly to South Bend to interview seniors for opportunities to serve as year-long volunteers after graduation. The university is nationally recognized for encouraging service among its students both during their undergraduate years and after graduation. More than 10 percent of graduates forego opportunities in business and other occupations to go off and serve our country and the world. I certainly know about that emphasis—I was inspired by Notre Dame's commitment to service more than thirty years ago and spent a year after school coming to Arizona to work in a domestic violence shelter and living in poverty with five other members of the class of 1984. That year impacted my life forever: I met my wife Sallie in our church's young adult group, married into a wonderful family, embraced the area's Mexican American culture, and have spent more time in Phoenix than any other place I have lived. It also impressed upon me the joy of serving the less fortunate. That experience living in a house with no air conditioning in Goodyear, Arizona, changed my life forever.

The most amazing thing about the process of recruiting students is the quality of the applicants I meet. The students are not only incredibly bright (it is very hard to get into Notre Dame these days) but also very passionate about making a difference in the world. While in college, I helped run a miniature golf course during the summer to make ends meet. These kids do medical research in Africa, learn second and third languages, and work in hospitals and law firms and Fortune 500 companies. They are bright, funny, experienced in world travel, and not intimidated about going to the other side of the world to help our children. Usually after finishing about twenty interviews for four or five openings, I am not only fired up about the people that will work at Open Arms but also about the future of our country and world. If young people anywhere are like the students I interview, our world is in incredibly capable hands going forward.

While they are at Open Arms, our Notre Dame students live, eat, play, sing, hug, study, cry, and laugh with the children who call Open Arms home. They become incredibly important members of our family, focusing on education first and everything else too. I know the children learn a lot from our volunteers, but I think the true teachers are often the children themselves. Our volunteers often leave as different people. They come to serve but quickly learn that giving often changes the giver more than the recipient. Our volunteers' love for the kids, dedication to service, and appreciation for life's blessings stay with them long after they leave us.

One of the things I like best about our long-term volunteers is that they live *with* the children. This is different than living next to them. The volunteers learn to overcome the boredom, monotony, and groundhog-day nature that living on a small hilltop in rural South Africa can bring. But this is healthy! Families the world over face boredom and monotony, and making such days special is what makes our volunteers so important. Whether it's silly plays they produce and direct, coordinating an arts and crafts project, organizing an Open Arms Olympics competition, or just reading a story to the kids, our volunteers turn everyday life into a rich and rewarding experience. They have the enthusiasm of youth, the confidence that people of achievement possess, and the spiritual grounding to help overcome the constant challenges they face.

If you are worried about the future, I can assure you that there is very little to worry about. If our Notre Dame graduates are any indication, the future is as bright as it has ever been. These young people just plain get it. They know that their mark in the world will be defined not by what they get but by what they give. They don't preach about God but rather do something that is far more difficult and rare—live out lives that give credit to him.

Thank you Patrick and Keaton ('11–'12); Anne, Anna-Claire, and Reid ('12–'13); Anne and Kevin ('13–'14); Kayla, Adele, Shannon, and Jim ('13–'14); Caroline, Brandon, Samantha, and Rachael ('14–'15); and Dan, Natalie, Janice, Connor and Mike ('15–'16). You remind us that a great education not only educates the mind but also the heart. Most importantly, you leave our children every year with the best gift anyone can give—you leave yourselves.

77. Lasting Joy

There are many things that bring joy to my life. Sallie is the best wife I could have ever found, and she has been by my side for thirty years now. My five children have provided the greatest joy I have known in my life. Together, these six people have brought deep and lasting joy to my life and will always be the most important thing to me, period. The beautiful thing about family is that they know our faults and weaknesses better than anyone, but they love us anyway.

But other, less important things make me happy too. I am a passionate sports fan, especially for the game of baseball. I played the sport growing up, went to college on a baseball scholarship, and taught the game to my son Sammy who is now pitching in the Major Leagues. I also love a good church service, a meaningful book, mowing the grass (yes, that is true), and a good glass of sauvignon blanc. All of these things make me happy and continually prove to me that simple pleasures are often the best kind.

But truthfully, there is very little outside of my family that has brought more joy to me than Open Arms Home for Children. It is an absolute privilege to be involved in this work because the children are so very special. There are very few things more heartrending than witnessing the suffering that some children live through. The children at Open Arms have been orphaned, or abused, or abandoned, or maybe all three. They have faced more challenges in their short time on earth than I will ever face no matter how long I live. But it is not the challenges they have faced that make them special—it is the resiliency they all show that is such a privilege to witness. It is one of the great joys of my life to see children who have suffered bounce back and live lives so full of love and joy. I am constantly in awe of the way these little teachers have taught me life lessons that would not have been learned without this project and resiliency is at the top of that list.

The great humanitarian Dr. Albert Schweitzer once said that "the only ones among you who will be truly happy will be those who have sought and found how to serve." That may seem to some like a high-sounding platitude, but to me it is an indisputable truth. I think it is the truth not because serving others gives us occasion to show the world how good we are. This is just self-service and does not bring happiness but the sin of pride. I think Schweitzer's words are the truth because when we serve others we learn that those we serve give us far more than we give them. It is not possible to give without receiving, and the receiving usually far outweighs the giving. This is why service brings happiness.

Ralph Waldo Emerson once said, "It is one of the most beautiful compensations of this life that no man can sincerely try to help another without helping himself." No truer words were ever spoken.

78. A Chance Occurrence?

Shortly after our family purchased the seventy-acre farm on which Open Arms sits, I went out to lunch in Phoenix with some clients, Mauro and Connie Florentine. Mauro and Connie are wonderful people and close personal friends. During lunch, I excitedly told them the news that we had purchased a farm to start an orphanage in South Africa. For us, it was the culmination of a dream and it was natural to share the news now that it was becoming a reality.

Mauro and Connie were excited to hear the news, not only to share our joy, but to tell me that one of their best friends in the world was a South African Catholic priest named Father Billy Barnes. They had met Father Barnes more than thirty years earlier when he had come to the United States to preach and collect monies for impoverished churches in South Africa. Throughout the years, their friendship grew, and they shared a lifetime of laughs, joys, tragedies, and vacations the way close friends do. Hearing the news of the orphanage, they promised me that they would call Fr. Barnes that very afternoon to share the story and see if we might connect on my next trip to South Africa.

Upon calling Father Barnes, Mauro and Connie told him of our plans to open an orphanage. Father Barnes asked if we were going to buy a farm to serve as the location for the orphanage. "Yes," said Mauro and Connie, "that's what Bob told us." Fr. Barnes then asked, "Are they buying the farm from a doctor?" Again, Mauro and Connie responded, "Yes, that's also what he told us." There was a silence on the phone, and Father Barnes said, "You're not going to believe me, but I just played golf today with Dr. Torch Dalgleish, a man I just met, and he said he was selling his farm to an American couple to start an orphanage. I had never met the man until today."

An elderly American couple knows one lifelong friend on the other side of the world. They call him, and the friend has just met the person who sold us the farm. With 45 million people in South Africa, what are the chances of that happening? With more than five hundred golf courses in the country, what are the chances of those two meeting on a course while playing in the same foursome? The odds are so long that I don't think it can be quantified.

Time and again, things like that happen in connection with Open Arms. So many chance occurrences have happened over the years that it's pretty clear that chance is not involved at all.

79. The Spinner in the Sky

When things go wrong in life, we often think to ourselves, *Why me?* This is a natural reaction to life's travails, and it is certainly understandable. Cancer, car accidents, migraines, losing a job—all of these things can get us to question why the big ol' spinner in the sky stopped on us. This has been part of the human condition since we started walking upright. I'd love to tell you that I'm not prey to it—"stinkin' thinkin'," as motivational speaker Zig Ziglar called it—but I most certainly am. I often get just as angry as the next guy when the spinner stops on me.

There is a big spinner in the sky, and as feeble human beings, we have no explanation for why it occasionally stops on us, our families, or on people who simply went to the beach for a tan and ended up getting wiped out by a tsunami. There seems to be no explanation for these things, just as there seems no shortage of people who seem to avoid the big spinner altogether.

If we question why the spinner stops on us—and we do—isn't it interesting that we often fail to do the inverse, namely questioning why the spinner *doesn't* stop on us too? For some reason, this attitude of gratitude is not as deeply ingrained in the human condition. Why was I born in the richest country on earth? Why did the spinner deem that I should go to college when 99 percent of the people on earth do not? Why *don't* I have cancer? Why do I have electricity and a toilet? Why *doesn't* the spinner stop on me is a question we simply don't ask enough.

The German philosopher Meister Eckhart once said that "if the only prayer you say your entire life is 'thank you,' that will be enough." I agree with him. If we're to be honest with ourselves in the United States, the spinner has stopped far more on people outside our borders than inside them. I know this because I personally know a whole bunch of children who had the spinner stop on them before they reached grade school. Interestingly enough, in their innate wisdom they don't ask why the spinner stopped on them. They just accept it and move on.

And so I ask, why don't we?

80. Full Surrender

Oscar Romero was a Catholic priest and bishop in El Salvador in the late 1970s. He stood shoulder to shoulder with the poor and oppressed in his native land, challenging the military rulers who ran the country to stop killing opponents and to end the suffering they were creating. It goes without saying that Romero's words were unpopular with those in charge, who repeatedly told him to shut up and effectively just "save souls." Despite the warnings, Romero could not let oppression and injustice stand, and he continued to speak out, often from the pulpit on Sunday mornings. He became a hero to the poor of El Salvador because he was one of the few people who had the courage to speak against the generals who ran the country.

On March 24, 1980, Oscar Romero was murdered while saying mass in the country's capital. He was shot by armed thugs who used machine guns to end his life in front of gathered worshippers. Killing him was the only way they could silence him.

I have a small sign at home that features a photo of Romero walking through a slum with words he once uttered: *"La fe no solamente consiste en creer con la cabeza. Sino en entragarse con el Corazon y con la vida."* In English, the words mean, "Faith does not consist of believing with one's head but in surrendering one's heart and one's life."

Oscar Romero paid for that conviction with his life. He was martyred because he refused to stop being a voice for those who had no voice. At some point in his life, he simply decided that he would rather die than live without speaking out for justice. He couldn't go about the work of saving souls if the people who had those souls were suffering greatly and unjustly. As he once said, "A church that doesn't provoke any crises, a gospel that doesn't unsettle, a word of God that doesn't get under anyone's skin, a word of God that doesn't touch the real sin of the society in which it is being proclaimed— what gospel is that?"

Full surrender to God's plan for each of us is exceedingly difficult. It means leaving much behind and risking all for the kingdom. Looking at lives like Romero's, we have to ask ourselves two basic questions. First, what am I willing to die for? And second, and much more important, what is it that I live for? If we can't answer the second question, then the first is irrelevant.

81. Two Words

In the four Gospels of the New Testament, there are many stories about the incredible deeds, miracles and words of Jesus of Nazareth. As a historical figure, Jesus has had a larger impact on human history than anyone else. Entire libraries could be filled with books about him, a man now worshipped as the Son of God by more than two billion people. No other historical figure has been as debated, studied or discussed. In fact, no one else is even close.

As a Christian myself, I often read the New Testament and books about Jesus. I have probably read more than one-hundred books that examine his life in one way or another. Some are worth reading, others not.

Despite the amount of time that I have spent learning about Jesus and the seemingly countless ways his life has been interpreted, there is a particular verse in the Bible that tells me as much about him as any book I've read.

The single verse I am referencing is contained in the Gospel of John. What's very ironic about the verse I love so much is that it's among the shortest verses in the Bible, consisting of only two words! But before we get to that, a little more context is required.

In the eleventh chapter of John's Gospel, we read a story about Jesus and his friend Lazarus. Apparently, while he's out preaching,

Jesus gets word that his friend Lazarus is very sick. For two days, Jesus goes about his business before deciding to go to Bethany, the town where Lazarus lived. Sometime during this period, Lazarus dies.

As Jesus approaches Bethany, Lazarus' sister Martha comes forward to tell him that "if you had been here, my brother would not have died." (John 11:21) Martha's words are a very heartfelt complaint. Martha feels Jesus could have healed Lazarus had he showed up before he died. She is upset he didn't come sooner.

Later, upon entering the town, Jesus is then met by Lazarus' other sister, Mary, who is crying and wailing for her dead brother. This moved Jesus, the Gospel tells us, and in the thirty-fifth verse are two words that I find revealing, compelling and worth celebrating. The verse simply says *"Jesus wept."*

Now you might wonder why the very simple act of Jesus crying moves me so deeply. That is a fair question. After all, crying for a dead person is a very common human activity. Almost all human beings do it at some point in their lives. What's the big deal that Jesus did it too?

I think the big deal is this: the two words "Jesus wept" reveal a man who knew what it was to be fully human, to feel so deeply for others that he would cry for them. By weeping for his dead friend and his family, Jesus showed the true depths of his humanity. And if he cried for Lazarus, he must cry for us too. This is marvelously comforting.

To me, this human side of Jesus is just as inspirational as his divine nature. There's a very simple reason for this: as a feeble human being I cannot pretend to know what it's like to be divine. I cannot relate to making the heavens and the earth, raising people from the dead or making miracles happen. Those things are way above my pay grade; I'm just a small and terribly insignificant sinner.

But, like Jesus, I do know what it is like to feel compassion for others who are suffering. I do know what it is like to feel the pain of others and to try to do something about it. I do know what it feels like to lose someone I love. And most importantly, I do know what it is like to cry.

To me, the two-word verse "Jesus wept" is more moving and more miraculous than what follows: the story of Jesus raising Lazarus from the dead! After he cried, Jesus went to the burial tomb of Lazarus, who had been dead for four days. As they roll the burial stone away, Jesus commands "Lazarus, come out!" and he actually does!

To most people, the true miracle of this story is Jesus bringing someone back from the dead. To me, the greater miracle is that God became man in such a way that he would actually cry and feel deep compassion for ordinary human beings. To me, this is more miraculous, more stupendous, and even more transformative than raising a dead man back to life!

When I read the two words contained in John 11:35, I know we worship a God who understands us. I know he cares for all of us in a way that once moved him to tears. This is worth celebrating! It is a wonderful miracle that Jesus could raise a man from the dead. This showed his divinity. But the far greater reality to embrace and celebrate is that he cried for a friend. Even though he was God, he knew what it meant to be one of us. Now, that's a real miracle!

I have every expectation that God will raise me to life again after I die. This is the promise of our Christian faith and we do nothing to merit it. Rather, it is a direct gift from God. But in an important way, I believe that eternal life is possible because God is filled with compassion for us, having experienced first-hand what it is to be a human being. He loves us, cares for us, and even cries for us.

Reading "Jesus wept" makes me cry. Not tears of sadness but of deep and abiding joy.

82. Challenges

Like every institution I know, Open Arms has faced serious challenges in its short history. We have had abrupt and unwelcome changes in leadership, been victimized by theft, had fender benders, had our grounds catch on fire, endured the death of a child, been short on funds at times, and battled a myriad of bureaucratic issues on both sides of the Atlantic. The list of challenges is long, and a solved issue is usually replaced with a new and unforeseen obstacle.

Despite these challenges and the frustration they create, we have never once thought of giving up. It has never entered our minds for only one reason: the children we serve deserve better. There is simply no way a person with even an ounce of compassion could meet our children and then give up on them. They have faced adversity beyond any bureaucracy or financial bind. They have lost their families and have found themselves all alone in the world. And yet they move forward each day with joy and resiliency.

The little teachers in my life constantly show me what *not quitting* is all about. And one thing is very certain: they are far, far stronger than any challenge we face. If they don't give up, then how can we?

83. The Rainbow Connection

There is a song made famous by the Muppets called "The Rainbow Connection." The song is sung by Kermit the Frog, and I have loved it since I first heard it during a year of volunteer service after college, working in the barrios of South Phoenix. The man who introduced the song to me was the priest who married Sallie and I, Fr. John Fitzgerald, a man known to most as "Father Fitz" or just plain "Fitz." In 1984, Fitz co-founded a homeless ministry in Phoenix known as Andre House, which is thriving to this day. One day I visited him, and I was struck by the fact that here was this giant Irish priest listening to a song by Kermit the Frog. It seemed an odd mix of man and music.

Fitz told me that he loved the song because of its emphasis on the magic of dreams, on the power of calling in our lives, and on the indisputable fact that that doers of special things are also dreamers of special dreams. Given his dream and work to start a ministry to improve the lives of the homeless, I could see why he loved the song. In it, the kindred spirits that make up the "rainbow connection" are identified by Kermit as "the lovers, the dreamers, and me."

Since seeing Fr. Fitz first sing the song with gusto on a hot summer day, I have come to realize that the song has a depth of spirit that is uncommon, especially in a children's song. In my favorite part of the song, Kermit sings, "Have you been half asleep, and have you heard voices? I've heard them calling my name. Is this the sweet sound that calls the young sailors? The voice may be one in the same. I've heard it too many times to ignore it. It's something I'm supposed to be." How many children's songs have messages about calling and the special regard we should have for dreamers and lovers? We need more children's songs like that. We need more adult songs like that. (My iPod has the song, not sung by Kermit because that is not on iTunes, but by Willie Nelson in a wonderful acoustic version).

After decades of occasionally listening to the song, it still speaks to me, and I know it helped give rise to Open Arms. Sallie and I dreamed about doing something like this as young newlyweds, and today we are blessed to be living a dream that is made possible by a number of people who believe in the power of "The Rainbow Connection," even if they haven't even heard the song.

Last night, all of us at Open Arms got together for one of the more important rituals we have, Friday night movie night. Every Friday after dinner, all of the children and staff gather to watch a movie on DVD. We used to do this in our cramped TV lounge, which is the size of most any living room. Now we do it in Emmanuel Hall, our dining hall, where movies are shown on the wall like a miniature theater. Popcorn is usually thrown in, and it is a special night to stay up a little later than usual after a week of school. As a result, missing movie night due to poor behavior during the previous week can be one of the most grievous penalties on our campus. No one ever likes to miss movie night.

On this particular night, the movie was *The Muppets,* and as usual, I had two or three children on my lap for the show. At the climax of the movie, Kermit the Frog took the stage and sang "The Rainbow Connection." After nearly three decades of hearing the song, it was the first time I had seen the movie and witnessed the song being sung by the wisest frog the planet has ever known. Of course, I immediately started crying, realizing that the words of the song had actually come true. The dream of a married couple opening a children's home was confirmed now by the three orphaned children sitting on my lap, all of whom wondered why there were tears streaming down my face during a Muppet movie. I told them to keep watching the show. Some things are better left unsaid.

I believe there is a rainbow connection. It is made up of people who dream and then do with love in their hearts. They listen to the voice inside them and then do something about it. I have been inspired by many such people in my life. They come in all shapes and sizes and faiths. They are connected by a rainbow that even they cannot see. Instead, they carry it in their hearts, believing it is real and acting that way too.

The song ends by promising a reunion that the dreamers and lovers will have one day. In my mind, this is the promise of our faith. It's also the promise of a frog made out of green felt who isn't afraid to sing of such things if only we'll listen.

84. One More Day

Several years ago, a country music group named Diamond Rio came out with a song named "One More Day." I love the song. It's basically about what a person would do if they just had one more day with a lost loved one. The song is partly about the pain caused by the absence of a person close to your heart and partly about what we might exchange in order to spend just one more day with them. I particularly love the song because it conveys the importance of not taking time or people for granted. The message is one we all should reflect on every single day.

My mother was a person who lived out the message of "One More Day" decades before the song came out. My mom frequently gave talks to churches and civic groups about enjoying life and not missing the forest for the trees in our lives. She was absolutely convinced that life should be enjoyed and cherished and that we all are on a wondrous journey if only we'd open our eyes and hearts to it.

On October 1, 1986, my mom got into a car to head across town to give one of her popular talks to a church group. She never made it. On the way, she was killed in a head-on car accident caused by the poor judgment of another driver. Knowing my mom, she probably would have found the design in the accident and instead celebrated the event as an opportunity to meet the wonderful God who created her. After all, she never did see the wisdom of biting into an apple just to look for a worm.

Now that my mother has been gone for almost thirty years, I think often about what I would do to spend a day with her. I think about what we might talk and laugh about. I think about how many questions she would have about her nine grandkids, eight of whom she never met. I also think about how much money I would give to have even one meal with her. The sum would be much higher than you would think.

When I reflect on my mom and the song "One More Day," it is very hard to not get emotional. It's hard to lose someone you love on a random Wednesday afternoon and not want some more time with them, even if it's only to say goodbye. More importantly, it makes me think of Sallie and the kids and just how much I would give to spend one more day with them if tragedy struck our family. What is one more day worth in such circumstances? I think the answer is always the same: more than we can ever know until it's too late.

In the Gospels, Jesus tells the story of a wealthy farmer who had such a big harvest that he decided to build more barns to hold all his wealth. Apparently, the rich guy wanted to save up in order to eat, drink, and be merry. But his efforts were in vain because Jesus says that on the very night he finished building his barns, his life ended. He never got to enjoy the fruits of his labor—or more pointedly, the spoils of his greed. For that reason, the Gospels plainly call him "a fool."

I think the point of this parable is not that it's stupid to build barns. I also don't think the story is about the foolishness of saving your resources for a rainy day. To me, the point of the story is the foolishness of wasting our time on things that don't last instead of things that do. To me, it's fundamentally about not using *time* well.

There are lots of examples of people who head off to the store for a loaf of bread and end up at the morgue later that same day. We often forget that, being too busy with the building of our own barns to take notice. But whether it's the words of Jesus Christ, the lyrics of "One More Day," or the example of my own mother, the reality is the same. Today could be the day that everything comes crashing down on us or people we care about and we start wishing for just one more day too.

No matter how big our barn is, nothing can fill the hole created by the loss of a loved one. Let's spend one more day with them now before it's too painful to actually listen to the song after their gone.

Believe me, the barn can wait.

85. A Letter from Bobo, Fall 2013

Nelson Mandela, the ninety-five-year-old patriarch of South Africa's democracy, has been in the news lately. His health is failing, and he has been in and out of the hospital for months. When he passes, the world will lose one of its greatest living treasures.

I have read several books on Mandela, and one of the central themes of his life is the importance of a good education. Throughout his life, he never stopped learning. Even while imprisoned on Robben Island for eighteen years, Mandela and his fellow prisoners spent a good deal of time teaching each other a variety of subjects. He also used that time in prison to study the language of his captors, Afrikaans, in order to better understand them. This dedication to education served him very well when he was elected president of the country in 1994.

Mandela once said that "education is the most powerful weapon you can use to change the world." He not only said those words—he lived them out.

At Open Arms, we bear a very heavy responsibility to educate every child to the best of our ability. This can be difficult when some of our children come to us at eight or ten years of age with no history of formal schooling. It is also the reason that we started a homeschooling program that focuses on getting children up to their grade level in intensive classes of two or three students. We started last year with twelve children in the program, and we are proud to state that two of our older boys have already tested into the best school in our area. We are doing our best to get the other ten children into good schools too.

To assist in this effort, we are in the process of building a new educational center at Open Arms. The building will consist of four classrooms that we can use for homeschooling, tutoring, homework, and computer-based learning. Most importantly, it will assist us maximize the God-given potential of each of the fifty-seven children who currently call us home.

None of this would be possible without your generous support. We thank you for giving our children not only a loving home but the great gift of a good education. We know that this will be the key to our children's futures, and it's also central to our mission to produce the next generation of South African leaders.

Victor Hugo once said, "He who opens a school door, closes a prison." As Nelson Mandela showed us, even being in prison itself is no excuse to stop learning.

Every child at Open Arms thanks you for blessing them with the educational wings that will help them soar as adults. We could not be more thankful.

86. He's Gone

On December 5, 2013, Nelson Mandela died. I shed some tears when I heard the news. The world has lost not only a great man and a great leader; it has lost a great light. Some people read history. Others make history. And once in a great while, some people transcend history. Nelson Mandela was such a man.

Mandela was a freedom fighter. He was a prisoner. He was a statesman. He was a leader in his country and on the world stage too. He will be remembered for all of these roles, and he should be.

However, in studying his life, I will remember him more than anything for being a living example of the power of forgiveness.

I don't know how a person can spend twenty-seven years in prison, be released, and then come out and forgive those who imprisoned him. I don't know how a man can forgive those who killed his friends and denied people even the most basic rights because of their skin color. I don't know how a person can invite his former oppressors into a newly formed government. I don't know how he could urge his angry friends, who were bent on revenge, to throw their weapons into the sea. Where does such strength come from?

Nelson Mandela is the main reason that the children at Open Arms have a future filled with hope and opportunity. Twenty-five years ago, such hope would not have been possible. Today, they live in a rainbow nation, and their rights are protected by the most inclusive constitution in the world.

Many people in South Africa speculated that Mandela would die this year on his ninety-fifth birthday, July 18. He died instead on December 5, the same day in 1956 that he was arrested and charged with high treason by the white government in South Africa. I don't think that's a coincidence. He died on a day that reminds us that good and even great things often come at terrible cost and after great suffering. Good things don't come easy. They come hard, usually with perseverance and sacrifice. I have been to Mandela's prison cell on Robben Island many times, and each time I come away humbled that such greatness arose from such a tiny, cramped, and cold prison cell.

While in prison, Mandela used to read from Shakespeare. He marked a passage from Julius Caesar that can still be seen in the book he read in prison: "Cowards die many times before their deaths. The valiant never taste of death but once."

Thank you, Nelson Mandela, for living such a valiant life and for being a light to all people, including fifty-seven children who have freedom because of your sacrifice and example.

You only died once, and you undoubtedly live again.

87. The Rock?

To me, one of the most interesting figures in the Bible is Peter, the Apostle. I find Peter interesting because he seems so much like all of us—incredibly human—that is, terribly inconsistent. In the Gospels, we read about how he drops his fishing business in an instant to follow Christ. We're not sure if we should admire his obedience to Jesus's call or question his rash decision-making. After all, who makes life and career decisions so quickly?

Later, we read about the time when Peter saw Jesus walking on the Sea of Galilee and asked to join him on the water despite the pounding wind and rain. We think how wonderful it must be to have faith like that, and yet it is hard not to question the foolishness of a guy who would get out of a boat in a storm. Just who does this guy think he is?

When Christ is arrested, we read about Peter taking a sword and chopping off the ear of a slave of the high priest. Again, do we admire the loyalty to Jesus or question how Peter seems to act first and ask questions later? In so many ways, Peter is a hard guy to figure out.

And perhaps most famously, we come to find out that despite Peter's love of the Lord, he denies even knowing Jesus when the chips are down. When it's clear that Jesus is going to be killed as a criminal, his best friend simply says, "Never heard of the man." So much for loyalty and friendship.

Despite the mixed feelings we often have for Peter, one thing is clear in the Gospels: Jesus loved Peter deeply and completely. Christ even told Peter that upon his shoulders the entire church would be built. I have to imagine Jesus told Peter this even though he already knew Peter would later deny him at crunch time.

The biggest takeaway that I have when reading about Peter is that he seems like a bit of a knucklehead. But God used him to start the Christian faith anyway. There were only a handful of Christians when Jesus died. Today, there are more than two billion Christians on earth. Peter—part rock, part knucklehead—was instrumental in turning Christianity from a small group to a major force in the world.

For those of us who profess to be Christians, I believe the key lesson of Peter's life is clear: God uses broken people to get his work done. Peter shows us that you don't have to be perfect to carry out God's plan of salvation. If so, Peter never would have been the object of Christ's deep love nor given so much responsibility. Perhaps it was Peter's role as a loveable knucklehead that caused Jesus to love him so much. Human flaws can be endearing, especially when they are found in good-hearted people.

One of the greatest traits of our God is that he uses flawed people to advance his purposes. He uses our brokenness to make things whole. He knows our weaknesses but uses our strengths to keep the ball moving forward. If you don't believe it, just read about Peter. He seems to have had more ups and downs than a roller coaster, but he played one of the most important roles in the history of the Christian church.

If God can use a guy like that to build his church, then how can we discount our own role in God's plan? As fellow knuckleheads ourselves, I don't think we can.

88. Our True Essence

It has always been interesting to me that the most universal symbol for the Christian faith is a cross. While it certainly is understandable as a symbol—Christ died on a cross to save people from their sins—I have long thought that the cross as the main symbol of Christianity is just a bit misplaced. And for this thought, I don't want to be considered blasphemous or a heretic. Let me explain.

When we focus on the cross as the ultimate symbol for Christianity, there is a danger that we can come to believe all too easily that life is meant to be little more than a patient endurance of suffering. The cross reminds us that life often ends up badly and that even good people like Christ often get stuck with unbearable suffering in the end. After all, life seems to have little point when even the good guys get killed. What point is there to living a good life if you'll just end up being on the very short end of the stick, like Jesus? He did nothing wrong and got killed for it. We sin every day. What will be our end result? With the suffering of the cross as our focus, it can all seem pretty hopeless.

Now, this is not to say that I don't believe that Jesus's death on the cross was not part of God's plan. After all, there can be no Easter Sunday without Good Friday, no rising from the dead without the pain of his death for our sake. And Lord knows (pardon the pun) that we ought to honor a man who would die for us. Not "us" in the collective sense but "us" in the literal sense. Jesus got tortured, whipped, and nailed through the hands and feet for us—*actually* you and me—and for our mothers-in-law, the Muslim down the street, and the gay couple who just moved in next door. Christ was executed on the ancient version of an electric chair for every single soul who lives today, whether we like them or not. That Christ would do this is worth celebrating, worth remembering, and worth honoring, but it was not upon the sad and tragic events of Good Friday that the Christian Church came into being. The ultimate basis for our faith came three days later.

When Christ conquered death by rising from the dead on Easter Sunday, he proved that we are not primarily a crucifixion people but something far more important—we are a people of resurrection. And when we realize this, our entire focus becomes different. Suffering is put in its place as part of our earthly condition, but it is by no means the ultimate reality we face. What we really face as believers is the *conquering* of death and the opportunity to live with God forever in the place Jesus called paradise. Resurrection means there really is no death and that anything is possible! This changes everything.

If the cross reminds us of this reality of eternal life, then I believe it is serving its ultimate purpose. But if it takes our focus off of Easter and the absolute joy it should be to live as Christians who are promised that we can live with God forever, then perhaps we should refocus our eyes and, more importantly, our souls on the true essence of who we really are. Yes, we are people saved by the cross, but more importantly we are people given never-ending life by a Savior who walked out of his burial tomb one Sunday morning. Prior to Christ, lots of innocent people had been executed unjustly. But none of them rose from the dead. It is a singularly unique event in human history and merits our focus in a way that the crucifixion cannot.

Jesus did not say, "I am the crucifixion and the life." He said, "I am the resurrection and the life." The difference between the two is not simply a matter of semantics. It speaks to who we are as Christians. Like Christ, we live our lives in the muck and pain of the human condition, but we keep our eyes on the joy and peace that only resurrection can provide.

Christians should be celebratory every day for the promise of living forever with God. We do not die! This truth should take our eyes off the cross and the earthly pain that inevitably comes our way. The promise of our faith is not ultimately crucifixion, it is resurrection. And it is only by God's saving grace that it is so.

89. At the Dump

Often on trips to Open Arms, I take along a visitor or two from the States so they can see what we're doing and hopefully become advocates of our work when they return home. We are not a big organization that can afford infomercials on TV or mass mailings, so this is an important way we can spread awareness about what we're doing.

In February 2009, I took Dave Nelson, an Open Arms board member and former professional baseball player, along with me. Like all of our board members, Dave is a wonderful human being and deeply committed to this cause. He is a longtime friend who has done much to help our kids, including hosting a charity golf tournament in Milwaukee each year. If there is a better person in the world than Dave Nelson, I haven't met him or her.

While on the trip, Dave and I went to a local town named Butterworth to see what was being done there for AIDS orphans. We are always looking for alliances and possible ways that we can impact the lives of kids, and the trip to Butterworth was part of that process.

In Butterworth, a local man took us to the town dump. It was something we will never forget.

At the dump, there were many people foraging through recent dump truck deliveries looking for valuable items or food that had not spoiled. Some of them were adults. Some of them were children. The garbage stunk, and the people looking through it were filthy.

The car went silent for a long time. We were thinking many of the same things and feeling the same overwhelming sense of horror that some people on earth have to do such things to survive. It was simply too much. No words needed to be said.

Dave and I will never forget that drive through the dump. We will never forget that some people have to climb through stinking garbage to survive. We will never forget how blessed we are to have been born in a country where such things are rarely seen.

I do not know why some of us are born in places with running water, nice beds, and plenty of food while some others are born where scavenging for food at a dump is the only way to survive. But I do know this: once you have witnessed such a thing, you are never the same. The images you see become seared into your mind, and if you are really paying attention, they remain in your soul too. Once they stir your soul, they change what you do. This is the most important change of all.

90. Fear and Love

Fear—not hate—is the greatest impediment to love. Fear casts doubt, creates judgment, and separates human beings from one another. Where there is fear, there cannot be true love, because fear makes human beings hold back. People cannot fully embrace that which makes them afraid.

Love, by its very nature, can only be fully expressed in the absence of fear. We cannot fully embrace that which makes us fearful. It is not possible to love entirely if that very act makes us afraid. Because genuine love is unconditional, it cannot stand the test of anything being held back. It is all or it is nothing.

I believe that one of the most important lines in the Bible is found in 1 John 4:18: "There is no fear in love."

We cannot be afraid of the guy down the street who looks differently than us, who worships differently than us, who believes differently than us. He is our brother, and we can only love him if we stop fearing him first.

Human beings are a reflection of God only when they love, not when they fear.

As people of faith, we are called to be a living embodiment of our Creator. God loves everyone utterly and completely. He is afraid of nothing.

91. A Letter from Bobo, Spring 2014

On March 16, Open Arms celebrated its eighth anniversary. Eight years ago, a scared two-year-old boy named Sipho showed up needing a home. He was depending on us to provide love, food, shelter, health care, guidance, and a good education. For that reason, I'm quite sure that on the day of his arrival, we were more frightened than he was!

More than 2,900 days have passed since that day. Because we care for children around the clock, that's more than 70,000 continuous hours that we have been hugging children, wiping tears and noses, changing diapers, serving food, doing homework, playing games, and carrying out all of the activity that constitutes an "ordinary" day at Open Arms.

And yet, for those people who have been to Open Arms, there is nothing ordinary about the place. The central reason for this is because our children are not ordinary. Certainly, they have suffered much in their young lives. Some have been abandoned, some orphaned, some abused. Despite this, our children are as spirited as any human beings I know and are as free with a hug or a smile as anyone you'll ever meet. Their refusal to wallow in self-pity or to surrender to adversity speaks volumes about the resiliency of the human spirit and the value that every single child brings to this world. In so many ways, our children are great teachers to us.

Of course, none of this would be possible without you, our donors. You not only give from your need but often send along a note or letter of encouragement to keep up the good work. I find this ironic because you make the work possible in the first place!

Thanks to you, Sipho is a well-adjusted ten-year-old boy who attends fourth grade at a good school. His daily activity is pretty much the same as any fourth grader in the United States. But believe me, there is nothing ordinary about his life or his home. You have helped to make both extraordinary, and there is no way that Sipho nor I can adequately thank you for that.

In his native Xhosa language, Sipho's name means "a lesson." I don't think that's a coincidence. Thank you for allowing him to become one of the best teachers I know.

92. The Gift of the Present

For thousands of years, wise philosophers and spiritual leaders have been telling us to focus on the present moment. In other words, they urge us to live fully in the now and stop worrying about yesterday and tomorrow. More than 2,500 years ago, Buddha said, "The secret of health for both mind and body is not to mourn for the past, worry about the future, or anticipate troubles, but to live in the present moment wisely and earnestly." Two thousand years ago, Jesus said, "Do not worry about tomorrow; tomorrow will take care of itself." (Matt. 6:34). And two hundred years ago, poet Emily Dickenson wrote even more simply, "Forever is composed of nows."

Regardless of how this idea is communicated, deeply spiritual people have found it important to remind us that today is all we have, and if we embrace it fully, it will not only offer us peace but also a glimpse of God himself.

Of course, being present is a very simple concept to understand. We cannot do anything about what happened yesterday (time tunnels exist only in the movies), and tomorrow may never come (think heart attacks, incoming asteroids, or car accidents). All we have is right now; it's the only time when we can be fully alive. We can't redo yesterday, and we can't live tomorrow today. On a very basic level, everyone can understand this is true.

And yet, because spiritual people always remind us about how important it is to be mindful of the now, it is abundantly clear that it must be something we must need to be *reminded of.* That's because spiritual people realize most of us live very poorly in the present moment.

Think about how much we live our lives in the past. We usually believe that any current reality in our lives owes its origin to something that happened before. "If only my mom had been more loving or my dad less of a slouch, I might not be so troubled today." "If only I had been selected for that promotion twenty years ago, I'd be on easy street today." We all tend to live our lives as if we're prisoners to what has happened before. We continually rehash things that happened years ago and give them power over our lives today. Of course, that's understandable, because it's a lot easier to blame the past than be accountable to the present. If we're honest with ourselves, we have to admit that most of us are world-class experts on living life in the rearview mirror.

If we think we're held hostage only by the past, then we haven't considered the future. Even more than fretting about the past, we are always worrying about tomorrow. "When will I find my true love?" "How will I retire comfortably?" "When will happiness come my way?" We have so many worries about the future that it would take many volumes to record all of them. We worry about the future every single day of our lives. It consumes us. "Tomorrow … tomorrow … tomorrow" often dominates our consciousness so much that it leaves us only when there are no tomorrows left on the calendar.

This focus on the past and future is not about missing the forest for the trees but about missing the trees and forest altogether. We're usually too focused on yesterday's and tomorrow's trees and forests that we fail to see the beautiful ones right in front of us.

Alan Watts was a twentieth-century philosopher who was born in Britain and lived his later years in northern California. I have read a couple of his books. Watts often used the analogy of a boat to describe how we live our lives. As I recall it, the basic analogy goes like this: Imagine that you find yourself on the shore of a calm lake. You get in a boat with a small outboard motor in the back. As you start the motor and head out from the shore, you can see it is a windless day, and the still water of the lake looks like glass in every direction. As you leave the shore and travel across the lake, you survey all the different places your boat can take you. And when you look behind you, you also notice that there are ripples being created in the water by your boat. (I grew up in the "Land of 10,000 Lakes," Minnesota, so this is an easy scene for me to imagine).

According to Watts, there are three very important questions about this scenario. The first one is easiest: what are the lines in the water behind you called? If you've ever been around boats, then you know that the lines in the water behind you are called "the wake."

The second question is not difficult either: What is the wake? It is plainly the trail you leave behind in the water. It simply marks where you have been.

The third question seems simple but it is not: Is the wake driving the boat? In other words, is the trail driving the boat? The easy answer to this question is no, the wake is not driving the boat. *You* are driving the boat by applying your own energy and direction to the boat's motor. It is simply not possible for the wake to drive the boat. But to this last question, one could say, not so fast!

It's important to reflect on things like this scenario in our own lives. Is the wake driving the boat? If we're completely honest, the answer is almost always yes. We think that we would be successful today if only we had gone to a prestigious school or studied harder at the one we attended. Our wake is driving our boat. We think we would be happy now if only we had picked a different person for our spouse. Again, our wake is driving our boat. We know we'd be so much better off today if our parents hadn't been so dysfunctional. If only the damn wake would stop driving the boat!

Honestly, we often live our lives as if the wake *is* driving our boat. We let our past control our present. And because of this, we often don't take full responsibility for the present moment, much less actually be present for it.

The analogy begs for a fourth question: "Is the smooth water ahead of the boat driving it?" We would be equally quick to answer no to this question as the third one. The water ahead isn't driving the boat any more than the water behind it.

But in reflecting on this fourth question, we have to ask if we live our lives beholden to a future that may never come. There's an easy way to answer that question: think about how many things we have worried about that never come to pass! I can think of a thousand things that I worried about that never happened. Truth be told, we let worries about the future dominate our lives just as much as we do pains of the past.

All we have is right now. Jesus, Buddha, and many others have tried to remind us of this truth. And once we embrace it, it is one of the most freeing things imaginable. You mean I don't have to fret about all the crap that happened before in my life? No! I can just let it go? Yes! You mean I don't have to worry about losing my job or asteroids hitting my house? No! I just have to focus on my wife if she's with me or the sun shining on my face right now or the bird singing in the tree? Yep, that's it, and it takes more than a lifetime for most of us to learn this truth.

There is a lot of importance that human beings attach to names. Soon-to-be parents often spend lots of time debating possible names for their children. Organizations like Open Arms name themselves using words or phrases that connote their function. In human experience, names are very important.

In the Bible, God the Father gives us his name only once. He does so when he meets Moses in the form of a burning bush on the mountain. When Moses asks God for his name, God says, "I Am Who I Am." God does *not* say, "I Was" or "I Will Be." This should not be lost on us.

The present is a great gift—meaning it is a present! It's the only place where we can be fully alive. It is also the place where we can truly be free, because being fully present means we cannot worry about what was or what will be.

But more importantly, embracing the present is the only place where we can meet our Creator. We can only be with God—"I Am"—when we leave "I was" and "I will be" behind.

93. The Main Thing

Like any endeavor, running and growing Open Arms Home for Children requires focus. Focus is critically important because there are always many challenges to be overcome. Because I am the president of the organization, the challenges tend to rise to the top and often fall into my lap. There are personnel problems, audits, tax returns, labor negotiations, and thank you letters, plus the pressure to find new donors and to keep existing ones. There is the challenge of distance, of running an organization on the other side of the world. There are occasional behavior problems with our children, challenges in educating each child properly, and power outages, computer failures, water shortages, and car problems. There have been flat tires, vomiting in the van, broken windows, brush fires (literally and figuratively), and snakes in the garage. At times, there are shortages of cash. At other times, there are shortages of wisdom on how to best proceed. The obstacles have been many, and they keep coming at us.

Despite all of this, I never lose heart. And I try not to lose focus. This ministry is about loving children. Anything else is just noise. As long as we're providing the most loving home we can, obstacles are just hurdles to overcome before the next ones show up.

Loving children is the reason we exist. And because loving them is easy, seemingly difficult obstacles become less challenging.

Thanks to God, the main thing for us will always be the main thing. In Mark 9:37, Jesus says that "whoever welcomes one child such as this in my name, welcomes me." Each day, we try to welcome him with a hug and lots of "I love yous." That is our focus, and despite the challenges, we never lose sight of how important that is to the children.

Obstacles are just obstacles. Hugs and "I love yous" are forever.

94. Like Riding a Bike

....

Imagine you are a middle-aged person. For many of us, this is not hard to do. Now, imagine that you have never ridden a bicycle. You've seen others do it. The five-year-old kid down the street rides by your house every day. What's more, you just watched a TV documentary about China that featured a scene of what seemed like a million Chinese people riding down a city street simultaneously. Many of the Chinese bike riders you watched were elderly, much older than you. They seem to ride effortlessly.

Having spent most of your life watching people ride bicycles, it would be easy for you to believe that you could do it yourself. After all, if a young child down the street and an elderly person can do it, you would have to believe that you could do it too.

But one thing is important here: just seeing others ride bicycles or believing that you could do it would not be enough for you to *know* that you could ride a bicycle. To do that, you would have to learn to do it yourself. And once you learned to do it and could ride down the street like most everyone else, you would go from *believing* you could do it to absolutely *knowing* you can.

What's more, once you learned to ride a bicycle, if your friends repeatedly tried to tell you that you can't ride a bike, you would not believe them. You would absolutely know that you can ride a bike.

Even if you doubted it for a second, you could hop on your bike and prove to yourself instantly that you know how to ride.

Our relationship with God is like this. If we watch others worship God and are raised in a household where church attendance is the norm, we may come to believe in God. But belief is not knowledge. Believing in God is not at all the same as knowing him.

I believe that Jesus came to earth so that we could know God, not just believe in him. I think that's why God chose to become a human being. He wanted us to *know* our always-loving Father in a deep and lasting way. He wanted us to know God in such a way that nothing or no one could get in the way of that relationship.

I hope and pray every day that I will get to know God more and believe in him less.

I don't just believe I can ride a bike, I *know* I can. I want to know God in just the same way.

95. Getting Paid

....

I don't receive monetary compensation from Open Arms Home for Children. I never have. But to say that I don't get paid would be a great misstatement. I get paid in hugs and smiles and an occasional note from the children. That is more than enough for me, and it makes me feel very rich, even when my bank statement tells me I am decidedly not.

This past Father's Day, the children wrote notes to me in a book on fatherhood. The book and the notes in it arrived a couple of weeks later.

As usual, there were notes that made me smile and some that made me cry. But one of the older children wrote me the following note that made me realize that the compensation I receive is beyond value:

Dear Bobo,

I am honored to call you my father. On this Father's Day I want to wish you all the best. What you do for me and all the other kids is amazing and I can never find enough words to tell you thank you for what you have done for us. I thank you for showing

me the fatherly love that I never got. You inspire me in
every way. God bless you. I love you very much.

From -------

If I had to choose between receiving a pile of money or a note
like this, I'd take the note in a heartbeat. Some things have no price
tag, and their value can only be measured in the heart.

If I get money, I can spend it or save it. But I cannot take it with
me when I die. Love is not like that. It never dies.

96. Reflections

Mother Teresa of Calcutta was a towering figure in the twentieth century. This is somewhat ironic because she only stood four feet, ten inches tall. Her work among the poorest of the poor inspired the world over and led to her winning the Nobel Peace Prize in 1979. Today, there are more than 4,500 members of the Missionaries of Charity, the order of Catholic nuns she founded, who serve the poor in more than 125 countries. Her impact and, more importantly, her example continue to inspire countless people today.

A simple woman of Albanian origin, Mother Teresa began her work on the streets of Calcutta in 1948. Two years later, she founded the Missionaries of Charity, and in 1952 she founded a home for the dying in Calcutta in an old Hindu temple. She believed that everyone should die in dignity, even the homeless and destitute. In this home, called Khaligat (the home of the "pure heart"), dying people were brought off the streets to die with dignity. Muslims were read to from the Quran, Hindus were given water from the Ganges River, and Catholics were given last rites. Mother Teresa believed in the dignity of all people regardless of their faith or economic status, and she wanted people to die knowing they were loved.

When Sallie and I went to drop off our daughter as a freshman at Notre Dame in the fall of 2003, we went to a large convocation where the leaders of the university welcomed the incoming students and their families to campus. One of the speakers at the gathering, a soon-to-be senior named Keri Oxley from Ohio, urged the incoming class to take advantage of the many avenues of service that Notre Dame offered. She promised such experiences would change their lives just as they had changed hers.

Oxley relayed the story about how she had spent the previous summer working at Mother Teresa's home for the dying in Calcutta. After spending some time there, she realized there were no mirrors in the place, even in the bathrooms. She asked one of the sisters why there were no mirrors, and she was told that Mother Teresa felt that the only reflection in the place should come from the eyes of the dying people they were serving. There was no need for any other reflection in the home.

When this story was told, you could have heard a pin drop in the auditorium. We all felt privileged to hear such a beautiful story.

I have thought many times about that story and about how the truest reflection of ourselves should come not from mirrors but from the eyes of people around us.

97. Connected

I was never good at chemistry in high school. Some have a talent for it; I did not. In fact, the only thing I liked about chemistry was the sound of the bell ending the class. But regardless of my personal feelings, I do know it is important. Chemistry explains a lot about how our world works and gives us insight about the fundamental processes that rule our world. It's important even if most of us don't give it much personal importance.

If you took chemistry in high school, you may remember the chart in the front of the room called the periodic table of elements. The table contains more than one hundred elements found in nature and the letter symbol for each. Honestly, I have tried my best to forget the chart since my adolescence.

But try as I might, I cannot forget that number eighteen on the periodic chart is argon, known by the symbol "Ar." I think about this element more than any other, but frankly, that's pretty easy, because I don't think about any of the others at all (except when I don't have access to O, oxygen).

Argon is an inert noble gas, meaning it doesn't really combine with anything else and has very low chemical reactivity. In other words, it just is, and it isn't involved in a lot of the chemical reactions that occur in nature.

There are three very interesting things about argon, two of them being physical facts and one other bordering more on the world of spirit. These facts, like many things in chemistry, can help us understand our world and may even help us understand our place in it.

First, argon is the third most common gas in the earth's atmosphere, right behind nitrogen and oxygen. Argon makes up about one percent of the earth's atmosphere. This means that every time we take a breath, we breathe in literally trillions of argon atoms. This is not particularly groundbreaking news. We've all been breathing in argon atoms by the quadrillions every day since we arrived on the planet, and it honestly hasn't meant that much to any of us.

But secondly, and maybe more interesting, because our bodies don't need argon to survive, when we breathe it in, we breathe it right back out. The guy or gal next to us does the same with our argon, and we do with the same with his or hers. This is where it gets interesting.

Because argon has a life of about 2.5 billion years, the argon we are breathing in each moment of our lives has most likely been breathed by Jesus, Gandhi, George Washington, and some guy driving a rickshaw this afternoon in Mumbai. It has been breathed by the animals in the stable at Bethlehem and even by the dinosaurs before they decided to exclusively become museum exhibits. The late American astronomer Harlow Shapley once wrote that argon atoms we breathe are "from the conversations at the Last Supper, from the arguments of diplomats at Yalta, and from the recitations of the classic poets." Shapley was a lot better at science than me, and he knew the science behind the statement. Argon connects us with every single living thing that has breathed, that is breathing, and that will breathe long after we are gone.

When I think of this, I come to a startling conclusion: we are all connected in a real and concrete way with everyone who has ever come before us. As we breathe this second, we are breathing atoms breathed by Benjamin Franklin when he read the final draft of the Declaration of Independence. We are breathing atoms breathed by Pilate when he sentenced Jesus to death and atoms breathed by Martin Luther King when he delivered his "I Have a Dream" speech. We are breathing atoms exhaled from our great-great-grandfather and our deceased mom's and dad's too. Thanks to argon, we are all connected in a very real way.

Now, we can deny this science and claim it is bogus. We can also deny that we are doing a great job polluting the environment, and we can deny that the sky is blue. But I believe the science surrounding argon not only with my mind but with my heart and soul as well.

For the better part of ten years, I have been engaged in work to help children in need in a place about as far from my home as you can get on this planet. Since day one of this exercise, I have been as connected to those children as I can possibly be. I have felt the pains of their personal histories, and I have witnessed their joy at finding a loving home that our donors make possible. I have shared their laughter and their tears. Despite the great distance between us, they are in my heart every single day.

I have known for a long time that I have a spiritual connection with the children at Open Arms. I didn't need a science book to teach me that. But nevertheless, I take great comfort from science knowing that the chances are good that the argon I breathed today was at one time breathed by one of the fifty-seven children at Open Arms. It means we have a physical connection too.

Something tells me that if each of us thought a bit about argon every day, we might not feel so lonely or disconnected with each other. Argon might just make us less competitive and, better yet, less judgmental. Most importantly, we might just gain a bit more respect for the dignity of every human being. After all, we just breathed in the argon that once went into their lungs. And they did the same with ours.

Science teaches us a lot about our world. Argon is a good example of how it can teach us about who we really are too.

Whether we realize it or not, or whether we like it or not, we are *all* connected, and it is my deep and fervent prayer that we live try to live that way too.

98. Who Was He?

There once was a man who was very rich and lived in a mansion. He was a very successful doctor. In fact, he was such a successful physician that he became world famous. He lived with his beautiful wife and two children.

One day, he contracted a disease that did not allow him to continue being a doctor. As a result, he quickly went through all his money. He was not rich anymore, and he lost his mansion. Because he could no longer practice as a physician, he lost his fame. Quite sadly, his wife and children were killed in a car accident. He was no longer a husband and father.

All of the labels that once defined this man went away: he was no longer a doctor, rich or famous, a husband or a father.

And yet, the man remained. But what was he now?

All of us work our entire lives to accumulate things, to thrive in our careers, to gain recognition, to be important in the lives of others. And like the doctor, all of the labels we work so hard to gain can be taken away. And then who are we? Who is left?

Who is left is what we always have been: children created by a God that loves us all unconditionally. He is one with us. For those who know this, no label-robbing event can weaken them. They remain whole. For those who don't, no label-robbing event can console them. They remain broken.

No person is what they have. No person is what they do. No person is what others think of them. Like the doctor, those labels can change in a heartbeat.

Human beings are created by God and loved unconditionally. *This is who we are,* and in the end, nothing else matters.

99. The Last Chapter

Anthony de Mello was a Jesuit priest who was born in India and often traveled the world to give retreats and speak at spiritual conferences. He was a psychotherapist by training and was known as a spirited, insightful, and often humorous man. He wrote more than a dozen books on spirituality, and I have read most of them. He often drew on many different faith traditions in his writing, a trait which led the Vatican to warn readers of his books that some of the material collided with Catholic doctrine. To be honest, this made me want to read the books even more. I have long felt that we can learn a lot from different faith traditions outside of Christianity, and De Mello's work reflects that belief.

De Mello often used parables to explain spiritual truths. This is not unusual in any of the great faiths that are practiced in the world. Parables explain truths in ways that simple doctrines cannot. The story of the Good Samaritan, for example, tells us how to treat our brothers and sisters much better than just saying, "Help people."

I love so many of De Mello's parables. They are often laced with humor and always filled with meaning. Like the parables in the New Testament, they make the hearer or reader think of God or faith in a new light.

One of De Mello's stories reminds me of what I regard as one of the core messages of faith. In the story, there are two brothers who

238

run a very prosperous farm. One of the brothers is a bachelor, and the other brother is married and has many children. They live in houses separated by a lawn in the middle of the farm. Each brother has a grain silo behind his respective house. They split the profits and bounty of the farm fifty-fifty.

As the story goes, often the married brother stayed up at night praying for his unmarried brother. "This isn't fair. My brother isn't married, he's all alone, and he gets only half the produce of the farm. Here I am with a wife and five kids, so I have all the security I need for my old age. But who will care for my poor brother when he gets old? He needs to save much more for the future than he does at present, so his need is obviously greater than mine." Often, De Mello wrote, this married farmer would get up at night and, out of pity for his brother, take a sackful of grain from his silo, go across the yard, and add it to his brother's granary.

The bachelor farmer, De Mello wrote, also suffered from panic attacks worrying about the welfare of his married brother. "This simply isn't fair. My brother has a wife and five kids, and he gets only half the produce of the land. Now, I have no one except myself to support. So is it just that my poor brother, whose need is obviously greater than mine, should receive exactly as much as I do?" Then he would get out of bed and take a sackful of his own grain and put it in his brother's granary.

One very dark night, the brothers each got out of bed filled with compassion for the other and accidentally ran into each other in the middle of the yard, each carrying a sack of grain on his back!

De Mello concludes the parable by saying that many years later, after the brothers died, their story got out. When the local townsfolk wanted to build a church in the area, they chose to build the church on the exact spot where the brothers had met, "*for they could not think of any place in town that was holier than that one.*"

"The important religious distinction," De Mello wrote, "is not between those who worship and those who do not worship but those who love and those who don't."

I cannot add anything worth writing to that.

Afterword

Thank you for reading this book. I am pleased to donate 20 percent of any profits generated to help the children at Open Arms.

Please keep our children in your prayers. I believe with all my heart that your prayers will make a difference for us. And if you wish to make a donation, feel free to go to *www.openarmshome.com* or send a contribution to Open Arms Home for Children, PO Box 2198, Litchfield Park, AZ 85340. Our growing ministry requires growing resources, and we would be most grateful for your help.

Lastly, I hope that you will find service to those in need to be as rewarding for you as it has been for me and my family. I am sure you will find, like we have, that the brightest lights do indeed come from the darkest places.

Sources

....

All italics in quotations have been added by the author and are not in the original unless otherwise noted. Scripture quotations are from the *New American Bible* unless indicated otherwise.

Preface

13: *"Fools for Christ"*: 1 Corinthians 4:10
13: *Mother Teresa:* Quoted in Richard Stearns, *The Hole in the Gospel,* Nashville: Thomas Nelson, 2009, 60.
18: *Rabindranath Tagore:* BrainyQuote.com. Xplore Inc., 2015. 3 January 2015.
19: *Black Elk:* BrainyQuote.com. Xplore Inc., 2015. 3 January 2015.
20: *Egan:* Quoted in Jeremy and Jim Langford, *The Spirit of Notre Dame,* New York: Doubleday, 2005, 117.

Chapter 4: Faith to Move Mountains

36: *New York Times:* Anahad O'Connor, *African Orphans Give Their All, in Song, for New Home."* New York Times, May 7, 2005.
36: *We Are Together:* HBO Documentary, RISE Films, Paul Taylor, Director, 2006.

36: *"If you have faith the size of a mustard seed"*: Matthew 17:20.

Chapter 7: The Rocking Chair

47: *Jung:* Carl Jung, *Synchronicity: An Acausal Connecting Principle*, New York: Routledge, 1985, 17.
48: "All things are possible": Matthew 19:26
49: *Mundakel:* T.T. Mundakel, *Blessed Mother Teresa*, Ligouri, MO: Ligouri, 1998, 85.

Chapter 13: The Only Bible Some People Will Ever Read

65: *Fuller:* BrainyQuote.com. Xplore Inc., 2015. 3 January 2015.

Chapter 17: A Great Truth

74: *Zevon:* Warren Zevon, *The Late Show with David Letterman*. CBS, October 30, 2002. Television.
75: *Zevon:* Warren Zevon, *Keep Me in Your Heart*, Dir. Nick Reed, Perf. Warren Zevon, Bridgette Burr, Ry Cooder, VH1, 2003. Documentary.

Chapter 19: Shoes

84: *Daily Dispatch:* Mapham, Tom. *Alone and Hungry.* Daily Dispatch, East London, South Africa, July 25, 2006. Print.

Chapter 20: Under Starry Skies

90: *Wiesel:* Elie Wiesel. *Night.* New York: Avon, 1960, 14.

Chapter 21: Six Powerful Words

91: *Borden:* Mrs. Howard Taylor. *Borden of Yale '09: The Life that Counts.* Philadelphia: China Inland Mission, 1926, 261.

91: *Borden:* Southern Nazarene University. *William Borden's Life.* Website. 30 September 2015.

Chapter 22: The End of the Road

95: *Ruskin:* John Ruskin, BrainyQuote.com. Xplore Inc., 2015. 3 January 2015.
98: *Mandela:* Nelson Mandela, *Long Walk to Freedom,* New York: Little, Brown and Co., 1994, 625.

Chapter 25: What You Do ...

110: *"Whatever you did":* Matthew 25:40
110: *"When you refused":* Matthew 25:45, New Living Translation.

Chapter 27: Spiritual Poverty

116: *McMahon:* "Interview with Pat and Duffy McMahon." Telephone interview. 25 Jan. 2015.

Chapter 28: Yin and Yang

126: *Mother Teresa:* Quoted in Wayne Dyer, *The Wisdom of the Ages.* New York: Harper Collins, 1998, 261.

Chapter 29: Playing It Safe

128: *"Went away sad":* Matthew 19:22. New International Version.
129: *Guder:* Eileen Guder, *God, But I'm Bored!,* New York: Doubleday, 1971, 53.

Chapter 31: I Promise to Sing to You ...

134: *Train:* Train. "Marry Me." By Pat Monahan. Save Me, San Francisco. Columbia, 2010. CD.

Chapter 34: Generosity

143: *Henderson:* Wesley Henderson. *Under Whose Shade*, Nepean, Ontario: Wes Henderson and Associates, 1986.

Chapter 38: Callings

157: *Schutte:* Dan Schutte. *Here I Am, Lord.* Anthology, OCP, 1981. CD.
157: *"Whom shall I send?":* Isaiah 6:8.
157: *"Who am I to go to Pharoh?":* Exodus 3:11
157: *What if they don't believe me?":* Exodus 4:1
158: *Wolpe:* David Wolpe, *Why Faith Matters,* New York: HarperCollins, 2008, 38-39.

Chapter 44: Imagine

175: *Einstein:* Albert Einstein, *Einstein on Cosmic Religion: With Other Opinions and Aphorisms,* New York: Dover Publications, 2009, 97.

Chapter 47: The Tension

184: *Schindler: Schinder's List.* Dir. Steven Spielberg, Perf. Liam Neeson, Ralph Fiennes, Ben Kingsley. Universal Pictures, 1993. Film.

Chapter 48: Woe Is Me—Not!

186: *Larson:* Gary Larson. *The Complete Far Side.* Kansas City: Andrews McMeel Publishing, 2003, 463.
187: *Dyer:* Wayne Dyer. *How to Get What You Really, Really, Really, Really Want.* Hay House, 2002. CD.

Chapter 53: The Children of God

211: *"Jesus called a child over":* Matthew 18:3.

Chapter 54: Religion

214: *Lincoln:* Abraham Lincoln. BrainyQuote.com. Xplore Inc., 2015. 3 January 2015.

Chapter 57: Good Tired

226: *Chapin:* Harry Chapin. *My Grandfather.* The Gold Medal Collection, Elektra, 1988. CD.

Chapter 59: Heart

234: *Rother:* Martha Mary McGaw, *His Indian Friends Kept His Heart in Guatemala.* Sooner Catholic, August 16, 1981.
235: *Rother:* Archdiocese of Oklahoma City. *The Cause for the Beatification of Father Stanley Rother.* June 27, 2012. Website. 3 January 2015.

Chapter 62: Faith to Move Anthills

247: *"Religion that is pure":* James 1:27
247: *"Amen, I say to you":* Matthew 17:20

Chapter 64: If You Want to Walk on Water

255: *Ortberg:* John Ortberg, *If You Want to Walk on Water, You've Got to Get Out of the Boat.* Grand Rapids: Zondervan, 2001. 31.
256: *"Lord, if it is you":* Matthew 14:28.

Chapter 68: Travel

275: *Third World:* Alfred Sauvy, *L'Observateur,* August 14, 1952. Magazine.

Chapter 69: Time Is Not on Our Side, Ever

279: *Freeman:* Dave Freeman. *100 Things to Do Before You Die.* New York: Taylor Trade Publishing, 1999, introduction.

Chapter 72: American Eyes

288: *Warren:* Quoted in W. Owen Cole, editor. *Six World Faiths,* London: Continuum Books, 2004, introduction.

Chapter 74: The Why

294: *World Vision;* "Global HIV and AIDS." www.worldvision.com, November 11, 2014. January 3, 2014.

Chapter 77: Lasting Joy

308: *Schweitzer:* Albert Schweitzer speech to the Silcoates School, Silcoatian, Wakefield, England. December, 1935.
309: *Emerson:* Ralph Waldo Emerson. BrainyQuote.com. Xplore Inc., 2015. 3 January 2015.

Chapter 79: The Spinner in the Sky

313: *Ziglar:* Zig Ziglar, *See You at the Top,* 25th Anniversary Edition. Gretna, LA: Pelican, 1974, 232.
314: *Eckhart:* Meister Eckhart, BrainyQuote.com. Xplore Inc., 2015. 3 January 2015.

Chapter 80: Full Surrender

316: *Romero:* Marie Dennis, Renny Golden, Scott Wright, *Oscar Romero,* Maryknoll, NY: Orbis, 2000, 97.
317: *Romero:* Oscar Romero, *The Violence of Love: The Pastoral Wisdom of Archbishop Oscar Romero.* Maryknoll, NY: Orbis, 2004, 41.

Chapter 83: The Rainbow Connection

326: *The Rainbow Connection:* Segal, Jason, Amy Adams, Paul Simon, Chris Cooper, and Andrew Bird. *The Muppets.* Walt Disney Records, 2011. CD.

Chapter 84: One More Day

330: One More Day: Diamond Rio, *One More Day.* Bobby Tumberlin and Steven Dale Jones. One More Day. Arista, 2001. CD.

Chapter 85: A Letter from Bobo, Fall 2013

334: *Mandela:* Nelson Mandela. *Lighting Your Way to a Better Future.* Johannesburg, July 16, 2003. http://www.mindset.co.za
336: Hugo: Victor Hugo. BrainyQuote.com. Xplore Inc., 2015. 3 January 2015.

Chapter 86: He's Gone

339: *Shakespeare:* William Shakespeare. BrainyQuote.com. Xplore Inc., 2015. 3 January 2015.

Chapter 88: Our True Essence

346: *"Resurrection and the life":* John 11:25

Chapter 90: Fear and Love

350: *"There is no fear in love."* 1 John 4:18

Chapter 92: The Gift of the Present

355: *Buddha:* Buddha. Thinkexist.com. 3 January 2015.
355: *"Do not worry about tomorrow."* Matthew 6:34
355: *Dickinson:* Emily Dickinson. BrainyQuote.com. Xplore Inc., 2015. 3 January 2015.
358: *Watts:* Alan Watts as told by Wayne Dyer, *"How to Get What You Really Really, Really, Really Want.* Hay House, 2002. CD.
361: *"I am who I am":* Exodus 3:14

Chapter 93: The Main Thing

364: *"Whoever welcomes one child":* Mark 9:37. Holman Christian Standard Bible.

Chapter 96: Reflections

370: *Mother Teresa:* Mother Teresa. *Mother Teresa Biographical.* Nobleprize.org. Nobel Media AB 2014. Web. 3 January 2015.
371: *Oxley:* Matthew Storin, *Spotlight: The Senior Who Inspired the Class of 2007,* Notre Dame News, October 12, 2003.

Chapter 97: Connected

375: *Shapley:* Harlow Shapley. *Beyond the Observatory.* New York: Charles Scribner, 1967, 48.

Chapter 99: The Last Chapter

381-84: *De Mello:* Anthony de Mello, *Anthony de Mello,* Maryknoll, NY: Orbis, 1999, 87-88.